Collector's Edition

The World's Greatest
Star Trek Quiz

Commemorating the 30th Anniversary of the Original TV Series

Intriguing Quizzes and Challenging Puzzles to test Your Knowledge of
the characters, places, and events that changed science fiction forever

Nan Clark

Mayhaven Publishing

Mayhaven Publishing

P. O. Box 557
Mahomet, Illinois U S A

Copyright 1996 by Nan Clark
First Edition-First Printing 1996
Cover Art by Loren Kirkwood
Printed by Bookcrafters, Chelsea, MI U.S.A.
Library of Congress Number: 96-077424
ISBN # 1-878044-33-8

This book is dedicated to Trekkers everywhere:
Live long and prosper!

Contents

Part II: Puzzles

Part IV: Scorecard

Part V: Appendices

Introduction

Star Trek lives! This fact is attested to by the never-ending popularity of not only the original *Star Trek*, which this year is celebrating its 30th TV anniversary, but also by the many movies and subsequent TV series that it has spawned. In fact, right now, TV stations, both in the United States and abroad, are still running the original series, often on a daily basis. They find that they can continue to air them week after week, month after month, year after year, to an ever-increasing legion of Trekkers, viewers from all walks of life, and from every age group. And why have these adventures of the first crew of the Starship *Enterprise* of the United Federation of Planets, set in a distant future, attracted this ever-growing number of avid fans? I believe that this phenomenon has come about because the stories and their characters have a universality of appeal far beyond that of traditional science fiction, and the characters themselves have truly become the Magnificent Ones, the shining examples for all future time.

Space is indeed a natural frontier, and the first Starship *Enterprise*, on its five-year mission to seek out strange new worlds and explore unknown civilizations, does present worlds of infinite adventure, worlds of action, worlds of the unknown and the unexpected among the farthest reaches of the galaxy. Like Arthur's knights of old, the crew encounter marvels, wonders, and enchantments, frightening realities and tempting illusions, the beautiful, and the grotesque, lands of both monsters and miracles. And like Arthur's knights, who come from many lands, the crew of the original *Enterprise* come from many nations and all races of the planet Earth, with the exception of the logical Mr. Spock, half-Vulcan and half-Earthling. These galactic space voyagers are on a quest to right wrongs and bring justice to the far-flung frontiers of the future. In their encounters with the forces of ambition and greed, with enemies often superhuman in their powers, they bring a definite and consistent code of moral and physical courage and a stubborn devotion to duty. These idealists from the integrated world of the *Enterprise* firmly believe that they can ultimately conquer the problems of an often troubled galaxy. And so imaginative is the truth of character and feeling throughout these stories that we, too, share this mystical belief that motivates the actions of Capt. Kirk, Mr. Spock, Dr. McCoy, Mr. Scott, Lt. Uhura, Chekov, Sulu, and the other members of this remarkable crew. Even the most formidable, the most grotesque, the most outlandish of the aliens with whom they must do battle are portrayed with understanding, often compassion, in the knowledge that beneath their external differences they are creatures much like ourselves.

The story of this new frontier, a place of seemingly endless adventures, of heroes and villains, is in its essentials a story of human nature and a story of faith in the future, a faith that there can be one world and ultimately one universe of peace and justice. And now the amazing adventures of Capt. Kirk and his dedicated crew are here to challenge you in a comprehensive book of quizzes and puzzles which are all based on the original T V series. Not only will you be astounded at its wealth of detail, but you will surely be able to astound others as well with your historical expertise.

Marianne O'Toole
New York City, April 1996

Part I: Quizzes

Ship-Shape

Here are questions about the *Enterprise*, the largest and most modern ship of its time in Starfleet Service. (25 points)

_____ 1.   What is her identification number?

_____ 2.   Who is her current captain?

_____ 3.   Who was her former captain?

_____ 4.   Who is the only crew member to have served under both captains?

_____ 5.   Who is the ship's chief engineer?

_____ 6.   Who is the ship's chief medical officer?

_____ 7.   Who is the ship's head nurse?

_____ 8.   Who is the person responsible for the over-all design of the ship?

_____ 9.   Who is one of the designers of the ship's engines?

_____ 10.   Who is responsible for the basic design of all the ship's computers?

_____ 11.   How much is the *Enterprise* worth?

_____ 12. - 13.   What two factors are necessary to achieve
_____   warp drive?

The World's Greatest Star Trek Quiz

_____ 14.   What is the greatest warp power the *Enterprise* ever attained?

_____ 15. - 16. What are the names of the ship's shuttlecraft?

_____

_____ 17.   What word refers to the principal method of recording time in the ship's log?

_____ 18.   What is the *Enterprise's* current mission in space?

_____ 19.   What is the approximate number of her crew?

_____ 20.   What is the name of the galactic organization which the *Enterprise* represents?

_____ 21.   What is the best protected part of the ship?

_____ 22.   What is the most common type of weapon issued to her personnel?

_____ 23.   What is the current captain's favorite place aboard ship?

_____ 24.   Where is Auxiliary Control located?

_____ 25.   How many science labs does the ship have?

Well-Schooled

The following are questions about the young Kirk and his Academy-related experiences. (20 points)

_____ 1. Who helped Kirk get into Starfleet Academy?

_____ 2. - 3. Where did Kirk conduct his first planet survey?
_____ What was his command rank at this time?

_____ 4. - 5. Who was Kirk's first commanding officer?
_____ What was Kirk's rank at this time?

_____ 6. - 8. What did Kirk encounter on his first deep-space assignment?
_____ What did Kirk feel guilty about as a result of this assignment?
_____ Which story recalls this episode in his life?

_____ 9. Which crewman aboard the *Enterprise* reminds Kirk of himself as he was 11 years earlier?

_____ 10. - 11. They were Kirk's two love interests.
_____

_____ 12. He was the teacher who many years later tried to kill Kirk.

_____ 13. Kirk had to study the works of this man, the discoverer of the space warp and an expert on space maneuvers.

_____ 14. Kirk had to study his works on military tactics.

_____ 15. His translation of the medical records from the Orion Ruins was required reading.

_____ 16. His history professor subsequently violated the Prime Directive and was assassinated.

_____ 17. This upperclassman always tormented Kirk. When Kirk met him again on the Pleasure Planet, he hadn't changed a bit.

_____ 18. This classmate later died with his ship.

_____ 19. He started out with Kirk but became a "dropout."

_____ 20. This classmate was killed by the Romulans when they attacked Outpost 4.

Mr. Spock

Lt. Commander: S 179-276 SP; lst Officer; Science Officer

This quiz contains questions about the "best first officer in the Fleet." (20 points)

_____ 1. Which one of Spock's senses is more acute than a human's?

_____ 2. Where is Spock's heart located?

_____ 3. What kind of blood does he have?

_____ 4. On what element is his hemoglobin based?

_____ 5. What is his normal pulse rate?

_____ 6. What is his normal blood pressure?

_____ 7. What aids his self-healing process in bringing him out of a state of unconsciousness?

_____ 8. What enables him to regain his sight after he goes blind?

_____ 9. What is his typical Vulcan life span?

_____ 10. Who aboard the *Enterprise* is in love with him?

_____ 11. How do Tribbles feel about him?

_____ 12. What Vulcan symbol does he wear on ceremonial occasions?

_____ 13. How long had it been since he had seen his parents before they came aboard the *Enterprise* on their way to Babel?

_____ 14. What is the official classification of his computer skills?

_____ 15. What was to be his destiny on Sigma Draconis VI?

_____ 16. What nationality did Kirk try to pass Spock off as when they were stopped by a policeman in New York City in 1930?

_____ 17. Against what person was Spock's nerve pinch ineffective?

_____ 18.-19. Where had Spock known Leila Kalomi?
_____ How long has it been since he last saw her?

_____ 20. Who calls him "Pan?"

What's My Line?

On the line before each name, place the letter of that crew member's profession. (25 points)

_____	1. Berkeley	A.	Psychiatrist
_____	2. Boma	B.	Navigator
_____	3. Chekov	C.	Crewman
_____	4. D'Amato	D.	Meteorologist
_____	5. Dehner	E.	Astrobiologist
_____	6. Finney	F.	Chief Pilot
_____	7. Fisher	G.	Communications Officer
_____	8. Gaetano	H.	Yeoman
_____	9. Galloway	I.	Geological Technician
_____	10. Harper	J.	Psychotechnician
_____	11. Jaeger	K.	Archaeologist
_____	12. Lindstrom	L.	Transporter Officer

_____	13. Masters	M.	Radiation Specialist
_____	14. M'Benga	N.	Sociologist
_____	15. McGivers	O.	Astrophysicist
_____	16. Mulhall	P.	Medical Doctor
_____	17. Palamas	Q.	Transporter Technician
_____	18. Rand	R.	Security Officer
_____	19. Rodriguez	S.	Records Officer
_____	20. Sulu	T.	Senior Geologist
_____	21. Tomlinson	U.	Botanist
_____	22. Tormolen	V.	Controls System Specialist and Historian
_____	23. Tracy	W.	Chemist
_____	24. Uhura	X.	Phaser Specialist
_____	25. Wyatt	Y.	Engineer

"Planet-Area"

The crew of the *Enterprise* discover many strange and exotic places in space. From the following clues, you are to name the planets. (20 points)

_____ 1. Only planet with which Starfleet Command forbids contact.

_____ 2. Planet presided over by the Caretaker.

_____ 3. Planet patterned after *The Republic*.

_____ 4. Planet which is the source of quadrotriticale.

_____ 5. Planet at war with Eminiar VII.

_____ 6. Planet known for its Cloud City.

_____ 7. Planet on which fraud is punishable by death.

_____ 8. Planet which is the home of the Vaalians.

_____ 9. Planet on which Spock saw dragons.

_____ 10. Planet on which the criminally insane of the galaxy are interred.

_____ 11. Planet on which Harry Mudd is taken into custody.

_____ 12. Planet which is Apollo's "Paradise."

_____ 13. Planet rated D- on the Richter Scale of Cultures.

_____ 14. Planet affected by Berthold Radiation.

_____ 15. Planet which is Trelane's plaything.

_____ 16. Only planet in the vicinity of the Murasaki Effect.

_____ 17. Planet which is suffering from the problem of overpopulation.

_____ 18. Planet which is Gorgan's domain.

_____ 19. The "Pleasure Planet."

_____ 20. Planet whose only survivors are mortal enemies.

Planetary Authorities

Name the person who holds the given title. (21 points)
And then place a "D" next to four of these people who die. (4 points)

_____ 1. Vulcanian Ambassador.

_____ 2. Organia's Chairman of the Council of Elders.

_____ 3. Ardana's Intellectual High Advisor.

_____ 4. Iotia's Chief Gangster.

_____ 5. Platonius' Philosopher-King.

_____ 6. Chairman of the Halkan Council.

_____ 7. Head of Eminiar VII's High Council.

_____ 8. Medeusan Ambassador.

_____ 9. Gideon's Ambassador.

_____ 10. Federation Undersecretary for Agricultural Affairs.

_____ 11. Tellarite Ambassador.

_____ 12. Sheriff of Tombstone.

_____ 13. Prefect of Argelius II.

_____ 14. Führer of Ekos.

_____ 15. Troyian Ambassador.

_____ 16. Assistant Federation Commissioner.

_____ 17. Teer of the 10 Tribes of Capella. (Name one.)

_____ 18. Chief of Miramanee's Planet.

_____ 19. Andorian Ambassador.

_____ 20. Proconsul of Planet 892-IV.

_____ 21. Cheron's Chief Officer of the Commission
on Political Traitors.

Clue Me In

From the following descriptive "titles," see if you can name the stories. They are listed chronologically, according to the season in which they first aired. (78 points)

First Season

_____	1. "Not the Salt of the Earth"	9/8/66
_____	2. "Superboy"	9/15/66
_____	3. "We No Longer See Eye to Eye"	9/22/66
_____	4. "Inside Out"	9/29/66
_____	5. "Split Personalities"	10/6/66
_____	6. "Artificial Beauties"	10/13/66
_____	7. "Sugar 'N Spice 'N Everything Nice"	10/20/66
_____	8. "Arrested Development"	10/27/66
_____	9. "Hot Seat"	11/3/66
_____	10. "False Face Feigns Force"	11/10/66
_____	11. "Noah's Ark"	11/17 and 11/24/66
_____	12. "The Play's the Thing"	12/8/66
_____	13. "Come Out, Come Out, Wherever You Are"	12/15/66
_____	14. "Where Dreams Come True"	12/29/66
_____	15. "Spock's Command Performance"	1/5/67
_____	16. "Son, Will You Ever Act Your Age?"	1/12/67
_____	17. "Diamonds Are a Man's Best Friend"	1/19/67

_____	18. "Déja-Vu"	1/26/67
_____	19. "How Do You Plead?"	2/2/67
_____	20. "Body Builders"	2/9/67
_____	21. "Brave New Worlders"	2/16/67
_____	22. "Fight, Fight, Fight,	
	Morning, Noon, and Night"	2/23/67
_____	23. "Sporadic Reactions—Even Spock!"	3/2/67
_____	24. "Mother Love"	3/9/67
_____	25. "Too Hot to Handle"	3/23/67
_____	26. "Either...Or..."	3/30/67
_____	27. "Missionary Visionary"	4/6/67
_____	28. "I've Got You Under My Skin"	4/13/67

Second Season

_____	29. "All Wound Up with No Place to Go"	9/15/67
_____	30. "God-Forsaken"	9/22/67
_____	31. "Symbiosis"	9/29/67
_____	32. "In a Glass Darkly"	10/6/67
_____	33. "A Garden of Eden It's Not"	10/13/67
_____	34. "Omnivorous Eater"	10/20/67
_____	35. "Pussyfooting Around"	10/27/67
_____	36. "No Wonder His Name Is...!"	11/3/67
_____	37. "A Change for the Better"	11/10/67
_____	38. "Getting There Isn't Half the Fun"	11/17/67
_____	39. "___ ___ Is Full of Woe"	12/1/67
_____	40. "Silver Threads Among the Gold"	12/8/67

Third Season

_____	62. "Goodbye, Crew! Hello, Love!"	
	"Goodbye, Love! Hello, Crew!"	11/8/68
_____	63. "Net Result: The *Enterprise*"	11/15/68
_____	64. "Mind Over Matter"	11/22/68
_____	65. "In Jig Time"	11/29/68
_____	66. "Feelings"	12/6/68
_____	67. "Weep No More, My Lady"	12/20/68
_____	68. "Madness Reigns Supreme"	1/3/69
_____	69. "Black and White or White and Black?"	1/10/69
_____	70. "Neither Sickness nor Death"	1/17/69
_____	71. "Now You See Her; Now You Don't"	1/24/69
_____	72. "All Aglow"	1/31/69
_____	73. "Another Time, Another Place,	
	A Different Name, A Different Face"	2/14/69
_____	74. "Headin' for the Promised Land"	2/21/69
_____	75. "Intellectual Heights"	2/28/69
_____	76. "Good Vs. Evil - Unveiled"	3/7/69
_____	77. "Two Different Worlds We Live In"	3/14/69
_____	78. "If I Were You"	6/3/69

Where It Happened

Match each event with the place where it occurred. (10 points)

___ 1. Life Prolongation Project   A. Deneva

___ 2. Bacterial Plague   B. Beta III

___ 3. Botanical Plague   C. Argelius II

___ 4. The Great Awakening   D. Babel

___ 5. Kirk's Peace Mission   E. Merak II

___ 6. Where Scott was an engineering advisor   F. Earth

___ 7. Interplanetary Conference Site   G. Ariannus

___ 8. Famine Rebellion   H. Axanar

___ 9. Eugenics Wars   I. Miri's Planet

___ 10. The Red Hour and Festival   J. Tarsus IV

Travelogue

Because of rather unusual circumstances, characters sometimes travel in unconventional ways or land in unexpected places. From the descriptions given below, name both the character and the story. (20 points)

1. He travels in a lidded box because one look at him would drive a human being insane.

Name: _____   Story: _____

2. He arrived aboard the *Enterprise* in a box marked "CLAS-SIFIED MATERIAL: DO NOT OPEN."

Name: _____   Story: _____

3. His masters used mind control to move him into their presence whenever they wished to be waited on.

Name: _____   Story: _____

4. As a result of her political connections, she was sent back 6,000 years into her planet's past, thereby dooming her to a lonely, cold existence.

Name: _____   Story: _____

5. He was removed from the cockpit of his airplane and beamed to the Transporter Room of the *Enterprise*.

Name: _____   Story: _____

6. Because he laughed, Charlie made him "go away."

Name: _____   Story: _____

7. For self-protection he removed his consciousness from Kirk's body and deposited it within the *Enterprise*.

Name: _____ Story: _____

8. He took a trip to Oxmyx's office by way of the *Enterprise*.

Name: _____ Story: _____

9. He was the first crewman to be hyperaccelerated.

Name: _____ Story: _____

10. On his mission to save Earth, he was the victim of the *Enterprise's* transporter interception more than once.

Name: _____ Story: _____

The Living End

In what way was each of the following forces rendered impotent?
Name both the method and the story. (20 points)

1. The Vampire Cloud Creature.
    Method: _____ Story: _____

2. The Creature that feeds on terror and inhabits a human
    being's body in order to kill.
    Method: _____ Story: _____

3. The M-113 Creature.
    Method: _____ Story: _____

4. Vaal
    Method: _____ Story: _____

5. The Doomsday Machine
    Method: _____ Story: _____

6. Nomad
    Method: _____ Story: _____

7. The Amoeba-like Organism
    Method: _____ Story: _____

8. The Flying Creatures whose tentacles enter the nervous systems of
    their victims whom they then control by means of unbearable pain.
    Method: _____ Story: _____

9. The Pure Energy Entity which feeds on hate.
    Method: _____ Story: _____

10. The M5.
    Method: _____ Story: _____

In Command

Match each captain with his ship. (10 points)

___ 1. Tracey   A. *Lexington*

___ 2. Ramart   B. *Beagle*

___ 3. Daly   C. *Farragut*

___ 4. Harris   D. *Exeter*

___ 5. Khan   E. *Astral Queen*

___ 6. Merik   F. The Tholian Ship

___ 7. Garrovick   G. *Constellation*

___ 8. Loskene   H. *Antares*

___ 9. Wesley   I. *Botany Bay*

___ 10. Decker   J. *Excalibur*

An Unusual Kiss

Each of the following embraces is rather extraordinary because of
one or both of the characters involved or because of an incident
which precedes or follows each demonstration of affection.
Explain the circumstances and name the story. (30 points)

1. Kirk and Shahna: _____

_____ Story: _____

2. Kirk and Uhura: _____

_____ Story: _____

3. Kirk and Dr. Anne Mulhall: _____

_____ Story: _____

4. Kirk and Andrea: _____

_____ Story: _____

5. Kirk and Ruth: _____

_____ Story: _____

6. Kirk and Dr. Helen Noel: _____

_____ Story: _____

7. Kirk and Lenore Karidian: _____

_____ Story: _____

8. Kirk and Miramanee: _____
_____ Story: _____

9. Kirk and Elaan: _____
_____ Story: _____

10. Kirk and Sylvia: _____
_____ Story: _____

11. Chekov and Sylvia: _____
_____ Story: _____

12. Spock and Zarabeth: _____
_____ Story: _____

13. Spock and Leila Kalomi: _____
_____ Story: _____

14. Khan Noonien Singh and Lt. Marla McGivers: _____
_____ Story: _____

15. Makora and Sayana: _____
_____ Story: _____

Firsts

Complete each of the following. (25 points)

1. The *Enterprise* is the first starship which ever collided with a
_____.

2. The first and only starship to visit Talos IV: _____.

3.-4. The first interracial kiss in an American TV series occurred between:
_____ and _____.

5.-6. "Each kiss is like the first" was spoken to
_____ by _____.

7. Pike's first officer: _____.

8. Ramart's first officer: _____.

9. _____ is about the *Enterprise's*
first experience in leaving the galaxy.

10. The first time Spock asked McCoy for advice concerned
_____.

11. The first person to achieve a mind link with a Medeusan:
_____.

12. The story which deals with Spock's first command:
_____.

13. The first person to bring a Tribble aboard the *Enterprise*: _____.

14. The first starship captain ever to stand trial: _____.

15. _____ was to become the first new member in the Platonians' Utopian Brotherhood.

16. The destination of the first star flight:_____.

17. The year of the first star flight: _____.

18. The first Vulcan on whom McCoy ever operated: _____.

19. His name is "_____the First."

20. Where Spock was really happy for the first time in his life: _____.

21. The first extra-solar planet visited by Lt. Galway: _____.

22. When Day said he didn't need any Saurian brandy, Kirk said the occasion was a _____ first.

23. _____ asked Spock his first name.

24. The first one to be killed on Taurus II: _____.

25. The first decision on which Kirk, Spock, and McCoy were in complete agreement: _____.

Numbered Places

With what person or event is each of the following associated?
(10 points)

1. Cabin 341 _____
_____

2. 3F 123 _____
_____

3. Encampment No. 1 _____
_____

4. 3F 127 _____
_____

5. 3C 46 _____
_____

6. Apartment 12B, 811 E 68 St., New York City _____
_____

7. Sector 39J _____
_____

8. Room 21 _____
_____

9. Starbase 4 _____
_____

10. 498th Airborne Division, Statistical Services Defense Group,
Omaha, Nebraska _____

Disease-O-Mania

Name the story in which each of the following diseases appears.
(10 points)

1. _____ The radiation sickness which causes premature aging

2. _____ Mass Insanity

3. _____ Sakuro's Disease

4. _____ Vegan Chorlomeningitis

5. _____ Synthococcus Novae

6. _____ Cordrazine Paranoia

7. _____ Berthold Radiation

8. _____ The water-binding catalyst illness

9. _____ Lacunar Amnesia

10. _____ Celebium Radiation Poisoning

I, My, Mine

Egomaniacs abound in the *Star Trek* stories. Here you are to match each character with his description and then name the story in which that character appears. (20 points)

1. Apollo   A. He believed he was evolving into a god.

_____

2. Garth   B. He planned on converting humans into androids.

_____

3. Charlie   C. He loved art and beauty and watching people fight to the death.

_____

4. Korby   D. He erased all ideas of opposition by making sure people "thought right."

_____

5. Khan   E. He considered himself "Master of the Universe."

_____

6. Mitchell   F. He wanted loyalty, tribute, and worship.

_____

7. Adams   G. He would lie, cheat, or steal to make a deal.

_____

8. Trelane   H. He thought of people as playthings.

_____

9. Mudd   I. He claimed to be a superman among supermen.

_____

10. Claudius Marcus   J. Beware, if you weren't "nice" to him.

_____

Food for Thought

Name each dish and the story in which it is mentioned. (20 points)

1. The kind of apples Gary Mitchell willed into being:

   _____   _____

2. What Janice Rand was eating when "Green" tried to take it:

   _____   _____

3. One of Scotty's favorite dishes:

   _____   _____

4. The Vulcan delicacy which Spock threw at Christine Chapel:

   _____   _____

5. What came out of the oven instead of the meat loaf the
   Enterprise chef put in:

   _____   _____

6. Kirk and Spock's attempt at psychokinesis failed to move them:

   _____   _____

7. Symbol the "space hippies" used:

   _____   _____

8. Riley ordered double portions of this for the entire crew:

   _____   _____

9. What the U. S. Air Force sergeant, who was beamed aboard the
   Enterprise, ordered:

   _____   _____

10. What McCoy recommended that Kirk eat in order to lose a few
    pounds:

    _____   _____

A Place in Space

Where can each of the following be found? (10 points)

1. Giant eel birds: _____

2. Blood-coagulating sand: _____

3. Series after series of androids: _____

4. Poisonous dart-throwing rodents: _____

5. Empathic mute humanoids: _____

6. Morgs: _____

7. Carbon-cycle rock creatures: _____

8. Anti-hallucinatory poppies: _____

9. Sandbats: _____

10. The total cultural history and scientific knowledge of all the Federation planets: _____

Bossism

Tell what kind of job each person has and then name that person's boss. (20 points)

1. Lethe   Job:_____ Boss: _____

2. Roberta Lincoln Job:_____ Boss: _____

3. Miss Piper   Job:_____ Boss: _____

4. Wu   Job:_____ Boss: _____

5. Drusilla   Job:_____ Boss: _____

6. Lars   Job:_____ Boss: _____

7. Jack Lipton   Job:_____ Boss: _____

8. Arne Darvin   Job:_____ Boss: _____

9. Mirt   Job:_____ Boss: _____

10. Alexander   Job:_____ Boss: _____

Once Upon a Time

In a number of stories, Kirk and his crew encounter people or creatures, experience events, or find themselves in settings which go back to an earlier period of time. How does this statement apply to each of the following? (10 points)

1. Zefram Cochrane _____

2. Atavachron _____

3. Yarnek _____

4. The Guardian of Forever _____

5. Black Star _____

6. *The Book* _____

7. John Gill _____

8. The Preservers _____

9. Dim Time _____

10. Empire TV _____

It Ain't Necessarily So

Despite appearances, there is something wrong with each of the following. Explain what it is and name the story. (20 points)

1. Kirk finds himself aboard a totally empty *Enterprise*:

    _____

    Story: _____

2. The supposedly mythical planet of Eden not only exists, but is exceedingly beautiful.

    _____

    Story: _____

3. Tombstone, Arizona, appears just as it was on October 26, 1881, the day of the fight at the O. K. Corral.

    _____

    Story: _____

4. There is no trace of life on Scalos.

    _____

    Story: _____

5. Gamma Trianguli VI seems to be a planet of extraordinary beauty, lush vegetation, and perfect temperature.

    _____

    Story: _____

6. Omicron Ceti III appears to be a paradise.

    Story: _____

7. To Yonada's inhabitants, their world is an asteroid.

    Story: _____

8. Spock is a member of the landing party which beams down
    to Sigma Draconis VI.

    Story: _____

9. The ship's computer record shows that during an ion storm
    Kirk jettisoned the *Enterprise's* investigating pod before the
    red alert sounded, thereby causing the death of one of his
    officers.

    Story: _____

10. Tribbles starve to death in a warehouse full of grain.

    Story: _____

Sons and Daughters

Name the offspring of each of the following. (15 points)

1. Amanda's son: _____

2. The Catullan Ambassador's son: _____

3. Christopher's son: _____

4. Eleen's son: _____

5. Finney's daughter: _____

6. Garrovick's son: _____

7. Goro's daughter: _____

8. Hodin's daughter: _____

9. Karidian's daughter: _____

10. Sam Kirk's son: _____

11. Linden's son: _____

12. Plasus' daughter: _____

13. Reger's daughter: _____

14. Starnes' son: _____

15. Tark's daughter: _____

Is That Really You?

Explain who each of the following seems to be, really is, and then name the story. (30 points)

1. Isis   Appearance: _____
   Reality: _____ Story: _____

2. Dr. Roger Korby   Appearance: _____
   Reality: _____ Story: _____

3. Vina   Appearance: _____
   Reality: _____ Story: _____

4. Dr. Donald Cory   Appearance: _____
   Reality: _____ Story: _____

5. The Organians   Appearance: _____
   Reality: _____ Story: _____

6. Nancy Crater   Appearance: _____
   Reality: _____ Story: _____

7. Balok   Appearance: _____
   Reality: _____ Story: _____

8. Flint   Appearance: _____
   Reality: _____ Story: _____

9. Losira   Appearance: _____
   Reality: _____ Story: _____

10. Karidian   Appearance: _____
    Reality: _____ Story: _____

Personal Attacks

Name the person who committed each act of violence as well as the story in which the incident occurred. (20 points)

1. She stabbed Petri.
   Person: _____ Story: _____

2. She scratched the "evil" Kirk's face.
   Person: _____ Story: _____

3. He broke Spock's legs.
   Person: _____ Story: _____

4. She tortured McCoy in a ring of flame.
   Person: _____ Story: _____

5. He tried to kill Kollos.
   Person: _____ Story: _____

6. He emitted a blue-hot flame from his finger and caused neural damage to Scotty's arm.
   Person: _____ Story: _____

7. He cut Kirk because of jealousy.
   Person: _____ Story: _____

8. He socked Korax.
   Person: _____ Story: _____

9. She poisoned Riley.
   Person: _____ Story: _____

10. He punctured Kirk's left lung with a knife.
    Person: _____ Story: _____

Officialdom

All of the following pull rank on Kirk.
Cite their action and name the story. (10 points)

1. High Commissioner Ferris

   Action: _____ Story: _____

2. Ambassador Robert Fox

   Action: _____ Story: _____

3. Admiral Komack

   Action: _____ Story: _____

4. Commodore Stocker

   Action: _____ Story: _____

5. Admiral Westervliet

   Action: _____ Story: _____

Of Therapeutic Value?

Name each of the following "remedies." (15 points)

1.   Prescribed for Sarek's heart condition: _____

2.   McCoy's antidote for the deteriorating effects of interspace: _____

3.   Given to Lt. Rizzo to bring him back to consciousness:___

4.   Taken by Prof. Starnes to rid himself of the "enemy from within": _____

5.   Necessary to preserve the M-113 Creature's life: _____

6.-7.   Supposedly administered to Kirk on Vulcan to compensate for the heat and thin air: _____. Actually given to Kirk on Vulcan to simulate death: _____

8.   Supposed to give its users more sex appeal: _____

9.-10. Given to Spock after his chest was torn open by gunfire on Tyree's Planet: _____   _____

11.   Given to Hanar to make him irritable: _____

12.   Administered to Spock to reduce his "attack" of Rigelian Kassaba fever: _____

13.   Dr. Lester's excavation party was exposed to this: _____

14.   Omicron Ceti III's "happiness pill": _____

15.   Injection given to Spock after he was attacked by thorns from a poisonous plant on Gamma Trianguli VI: _____

The Other Kirk

In some of the *Star Trek* stories, Kirk is "just not himself." From the following clues, name the story and tell why. (20 points)

1. Everyone in town thinks he's someone else.
   Story: _____ Reason: _____

2. O. K., now let's see you look like Kirk.
   Story: _____ Reason: _____

3. You two must get together.
   Story: _____ Reason: _____

4. Memory isn't one of his strong points.
   Story: _____ Reason: _____

5. Kirk, an entertainer?
   Story: _____ Reason: _____

6. If he's there, who's here?
   Story: _____ Reason: _____

7. I know appearances can be deceiving, but as a woman?
   Story: _____ Reason: _____

8. The Captain wouldn't talk like that!
   Story: _____ Reason: _____

9. Kirk really gave a lot of himself.
   Story: _____ Reason: _____

10. Like Spock?
    Story: _____ Reason: _____

Animal, Vegetable, Mineral

Identify each of the following. (10 points)

_____ 1. Kirk nearly died from its bite.

_____ 2. This animate, swaying, noise-producing plant must be hand-fed.

_____ 3. This inhabitant of Alfa 177 couldn't be put back together.

_____ 4. Darnell supposedly died from eating it.

_____ 5. Nona used one to save Kirk's life.

_____ 6. Scotty said that Lincoln was as "loony" as one.

_____ 7. Cyrano Jones tried to sell some of these stones to a bartender.

_____ 8. This high-yield, four-lobed perennial hybrid of wheat and rye originated in Canada.

_____ 9. Gary Seven came to Earth with one.

_____10. This crystal formation grows on Kelva.

Weaponry

Name the weapon. (10 points)

1. It drains the mind, leaving its victims feeling so helpless and alone that whoever is in control of this machine can implant whatever thoughts and responses they wish. _____

2. With this, one can monitor anyone aboard the *I. S. S. Enterprise* and then, with the touch of a button, destroy that person. _____

3. The landing party used this to overcome Norman and the other androids on Mudd's Planet. _____

4. With this mining tool, the Troglyte Disruptors mutilated works of art on Stratos. _____

5. Gary Seven used this device to neutralize phasers, remove a force field, and open and close locks. _____

6. McCoy had one of these implanted in his forehead. _____

7. Landru, Sevrin, and Kirk found this to be a very powerful weapon. _____

8. This deadly, primitive type of boomerang proved most effective on Capella IV. _____

9. According to Vulcan custom, Spock and Kirk were required to fight with this weapon first. _____

10. This device didn't work, although by all the laws of science and logic it should have. _____

In Other Words

Match each term in the second column with its equivalent meaning in the first column. (10 points)

___ 1. Eymorg	A.	Man
___ 2. Klee-fah	B.	Mating Time
___ 3. Radans	C.	Wedding
___ 4. Sentinels	D.	Children
___ 5. Replacements	E.	Woman
___ 6. Joining	F.	Witch
___ 7. Kroykah	G.	No
___ 8. Kanutu	H.	Guards
___ 9. Morg	I.	Silence
___10. Pon Far	J.	Dilithium Crystals

Mineral Deposits

Name what each of the following is used for, where it can be found, and in what story it appears. (15 points)

	Used For	Found On	Story
1. Zienite			
2. Ryetalyn			
3. Kironide			
4. Pergium			
5. Topaline			

To the Death

Each of the following dies in an unnatural way. Tell how and name the story. (50 points)

1. Marta _____
   Story: _____

2. Agents 201 and 347 _____
   Story: _____

3. Watson _____
   Story: _____

4. Harper _____
   Story: _____

5. O'Herlihy _____
   Story: _____

6. Galloway _____
   Story: _____

7. Wyatt _____
   Story: _____

8. Tomlinson _____
   Story: _____

9. Kras _____
   Story: _____

10. Prof. Starnes _____
    Story: _____

11. John Gill _____
    Story: _____

12. The Memory Alpha Technician _____
    Story: _____

13. Ramart _____
    Story: _____

14. Matthews _____
    Story: _____

15. Mallory _____
    Story: _____

16. Dr. Tristan Adams _____
    Story: _____

17. Lt. Lee Kelso _____
    Story: _____

18. Commodore Matt Decker _____
    Story: _____

19. William B. Harrison _____
    Story: _____

20.   Edith Keeler   _____
        Story: _____

21.   Dr. Thomas Leighton   _____
        Story: _____

22.   Louise   _____
        Story: _____

23.   Marvick   _____
        Story: _____

24.   Adam   _____
        Story: _____

25.   Thompson   _____
        Story: _____

Matrimonial Alliances

Name the woman. (20 points)

1. Akaar   _____

2. Benton   _____

3. Ben Childress   _____

4. Robert Crater   _____

5. Herm Gossett   _____

6. Jaris   _____

7. Robert Johnson   _____

8. Kang   _____

9. Sam Kirk   _____

10. Kirok   _____

11. Thomas Leighton   _____

12. Leonard McCoy   _____

13. Harry Mudd   _____

14. Parmen   _____

15. Jacques Romaine   _____

16. Sarek   _____

17. Sargon   _____

18. Spock   _____

19. Tyree   _____

20. Theodore Wallace   _____

Superlatives

Identify each of the following. (15 points)

1. The "sweetest creature known to man." _____
2. The most handsome face Kirk ever saw. _____
3. The woman who was "loved more than anyone else in the universe." _____
4. The greatest Vulcan who ever lived. _____
5. The "best-kept secret in the galaxy." _____
6. Kirk's most difficult task. _____
7. The hardest substance known to Federation science. _____
8. "Troyius' most deadly enemy." _____
9. The "galaxy's most destructive weapon." _____
10. The greatest piece of surgery McCoy ever saw. _____
    _____
11. The makers of the "sweetest little automatic in the world."
    _____
12. Spock considered this to be the finest example of sustained anti-gravity elevation. _____
13. He claimed to have invented the most powerful explosive in history. _____
14. The loneliest Spock's human side ever felt. _____
15. The greatest natural miner in the universe. _____

Thought Manifestations

With whom is each of the following associated? (10 points)

_____ 1. White rabbit

_____ 2. World War II Gruman Hellcat fighter

_____ 3. Flowing Greek robe & golden sandals

_____ 4. Don Juan

_____ 5. Encampment No. 1

_____ 6. Abraham Lincoln

_____ 7. 18th century dueling pistols

_____ 8. Samurai

_____ 9. Tango

_____ 10. Vegetation and water

Gifts

Name one gift each of the following gave to the other. (10 points)

_____ 1. Miramanee to Kirk

_____ 2. Trelane to Teresa Ross

_____ 3. Elaan's future mother-in-law to Elaan

_____ 4. Kirk to Vanna

_____ 5. Elaan to Kirk

_____ 6. Garth to Marta

_____ 7. Philana to Spock

_____ 8. Philana to Kirk

_____ 9. Philana to McCoy

_____ 10. Charlie to Janice Rand

Kirkathon

James T. Kirk
Captain, Star Fleet Command SC 937-0176 CEC

Who referred to Kirk in the following ways and in what story?
(20 Points)

Speaker	Story	
_____	_____	1. "Laddie Buck"
_____	_____	2. "Creator"
_____	_____	3. "Herbert"
_____	_____	4. "Mister Lovey-Dovey
_____	_____	5. "Captain Dunsel"
_____	_____	6. "James"
_____	_____	7. "My Chief"
_____	_____	8. "Caesar of the Stars"
_____	_____	9. "Jimmy Boy"
_____	_____	10. "Lord"

Ceremonial Occasions

All of the following concern protocol and tradition. (10 points)

1. What seemed odd to Abraham Lincoln about the ceremonial ruffles and flourishes that were being played when he boarded the *Enterprise*? _____

2. What is the significance of the Capellan custom of placing one's hand over one's heart and then extending an open hand?

   _____

3. At Garth's coronation what title did he give to Kirk?

   _____

4. Of what crime were those who entered the Oracle Room on Yonada guilty? _____

5. What is the call for a Vulcan marriage ceremony to begin?

   _____

6. What is the call for a Vulcan marriage challenge to begin?

   _____

7. What is the ceremonial place of a Vulcan marriage and challenge called? _____

8. What is a Promise of Silence? _____

9. Who participated in a Promise of Silence? _____

10. Describe the Vulcan salute. _____

_____

Assorted Quotes

Name the speaker. (10 points)

1. "What is ours is ours again." _____

2. "May the Great Bird of the galaxy bless your planet." _____

3. "All my life I've dreamed of being alone." _____

4. "He's got jelly in the belly." _____

5. "May we together become greater than the sum of both of us."
   _____

6. "We have no devil, Kirk." _____

7. "Our souls have been together." _____

8. "After a time, you may find that *having* is not, after all, so pleasing a thing as *wanting*." _____

9. "Command requirements do not recognize personal privilege."

   _____

10. "I don't know what I can offer against Paradise." _____

Life Savers

Explain how each of the following was in some way able to survive an almost certain death and name the story in which the incident occurred. (20 points)

1. Spock, from seeing Kollos: _____
   Story: _____

2. Gem, from McCoy's wounds: _____
   Story: _____

3. Kirk, from asphyxiation in the *Enterprise's* decompression chamber: _____
   Story: _____

4. Spock, Scott, McCoy, Boma, and Mears, with their ship: _____
   Story: _____

5. Kirk, from death at Spock's hands on Vulcan: _____
   Story: _____

6. The *Enterprise* and her crew, from being destroyed by Captain Wesley and the *Lexington*: _____
   Story: _____

7. Sarek, in order to stay alive for his operation: _____
Story: _____

8. Spock, from being destroyed by a flying parasite on Deneva:

_____

Story: _____

9. An unconscious Spock-2, from death in the Mirror Universe:

_____

Story: _____

10. Kirk, from death at the hands of Trelane: _____
Story: _____

Triangles

Each of the following is listed with the object of his or her affection. Name the person considered to be a rival and tell how the situation was resolved. (20 points)

1. Spock   T'Pring

   Rival: _____   Resolution: _____

2. Scott   Carolyn Palamas

   Rival: _____   Resolution: _____

3. Miri   Kirk

   Rival: _____   Resolution: _____

4. Rojan   Kelinda

   Rival: _____   Resolution: _____

5. Marvick   Miranda Jones

   Rival: _____   Resolution: _____

6. Billy Claiborne   Sylvia

   Rival: _____   Resolution: _____

7. Flint   Reena Kapec

   Rival: _____   Resolution: _____

8. Rael   Deela

   Rival: _____   Resolution: _____

9. Spock   Zarabeth

   Rival: _____   Resolution: _____

10. Trelane   Teresa Ross

   Rival: _____   Resolution: _____

Notables

All of the following have a position of some importance. Name what the person's job is and where each one works. (60 points)

Job: _____ Place of Employment _____ 1. Akuta

Job: _____ Place of Employment _____ 2. Ed Appel

Job: _____ Place of Employment _____ 3. Mr. Atoz

Job: _____ Place of Employment _____ 4. Ben Childress

Job: _____ Place of Employment _____ 5. Cloud William

Job: _____ Place of Employment _____ 6. Dr. Robert Crater

Job: _____ Place of Employment _____ 7. Dr. Donald Cory

Job: _____ Place of Employment _____ 8. Cromwell

Job: _____ Place of Employment _____ 9. Galt

Job: _____ Place of Employment _____ 10. Humbolt

Job: _____ Place of Employment _____ 11. Jahn

Job: _____ Place of Employment _____ 12. Leila Kalomi

Job: _____ Place of Employment _____ 13. Kara

Job: _____ Place of Employment _____ 14. Edith Keeler

Job: _____ Place of Employment _____ 15. Sam Kirk

Job: _____ Place of Employment _____ 16. Jojo Krako

Job: _____ Place of Employment _____ 17. Losira

Job: _____ Place of Employment _____ 18. Mr. Lurry

Job: _____ Place of Employment _____ 19. Melakon

Job: _____ Place of Employment _____ 20. Natira

Job: _____ Place of Employment _____ 21. Rael

Job: _____ Place of Employment _____ 22. Salish

Job: _____ Place of Employment _____ 23. Elias Sandoval

Job: _____ Place of Employment _____ 24. Septimus

Job: _____ Place of Employment _____ 25. Prof. Starnes

Job: _____ Place of Employment _____ 26. Commodore Stone

Job: _____ Place of Employment _____ 27. Tepo

Job: _____ Place of Employment _____ 28. T'Pau

Job: _____ Place of Employment _____ 29. CommodoreTravers

Job: _____ Place of Employment _____ 30. Vanderberg

Not On Friendly Terms

Name the adversary of each of the following. (10 points)

1. Yangs   _____

2. Earps   _____

3. Ekos   _____

4. Eminiar   _____

5. Morgs   _____

6. Krako   _____

7. Hanoch   _____

8. Lokai   _____

9. Akaar   _____

10. Elas   _____

Let Me Entertain You

Name the entertainer and the story. (20 points)

	Entertainer	Story
1. "I'll Take You Home Again, Kathleen"	_____	_____
2. "Beyond Antares"	_____	_____
3. "Maiden Wine"	_____	_____
4. "The Good Land"	_____	_____
5. A Brahms waltz	_____	_____
6. An Orion slave girl's dance	_____	_____
7. "Ring Around a Rosy"	_____	_____
8. "Tweedledee and Tweedledum"	_____	_____
9. *Macbeth*	_____	_____
10. "Good Night, Sweetheart"	_____	_____

"Of Great Mettle"

Name the metal. (10 points)

_____ 1. Composition of the Doomsday Machine.

_____ 2. Trace metal which when mixed in even the smallest amount with ryetalyn will destroy ryetalyn's effectiveness.

_____ 3. Composition of the knife blade which killed Kara, Karen, and Sybo.

_____ 4. Found in abundant supply on Coridan, Halkan, and Rigel XII.

_____ 5. Compositional alloy over which the skin-like texture of an android is placed.

_____ 6. Compositional alloy of the Kalandan Outpost Planet.

_____ 7. Needed to effect repairs on the meteor damage to the _S. S. Beagle_.

_____ 8. Composition of transponder crystals.

_____ 9. Alloy used in the outside hull of shuttlecraft.

_____10. Substance used to shield outpost stations.

Some Place

Tell with whom or what each of the following is associated and then name the story. (30 points)

1. Hall of Audiences _____
   Story: _____

2. Oracle Room _____
   Story: _____

3. Chamber of the Ages _____
   Story: _____

4. Negative Magnetic Corridor _____
   Story: _____

5. Zone of Darkness _____
   Story: _____

6. Interspace _____
   Story: _____

7. Chancellory Detention Center _____
   Story: _____

8. Here Above; Here Below _____
   Story: _____

9. Science Group Headquarters _____
   Story: _____

10. Division of Control _____
    Story: _____

11. Checkpoint Tiger _____
    Story: _____

12. Cantaba Street _____
    Story: _____

13. The Valley _____
    Story: _____

14. Sandara _____
    Story: _____

15. The Rostrum _____
    Story: _____

Nan Clark

Communications

In space, information may be disseminated in quite unorthodox ways. (10 points)

_____ 1. These are used in nightclubs on Argelius II to indicate approval.

_____ 2. The Eymorgs wear these to control their subjects.

_____ 3. This special kind of dress gives Dr. Miranda Jones the ability to "see."

_____ 4. Both Kirk and the Gorn are given one of these communication devices.

_____ 5. These devices are placed around the necks of thralls to warn or punish them when they don't obey orders.

_____ 6. This shipboard device enables the crew of the *Enterprise* to understand all alien beings.

_____ 7. McCoy learns how to restore Spock's brain by wearing this.

_____ 8. This device within the Beta Five Computer affects complex mechanisms at great distances.

_____ 9. The Talosians use this means of communication to reward or punish their subjects.

_____10. Gem uses this method to gain knowledge and understanding.

Poetics

Who recites each of the following and in what story? (30 points)

1.
> "All I ask is a tall ship
> And a star to steer her by."

Reciter: _____ Story: _____

2.
> "Being your slave, what should I do but tend
> Upon the hours and times of your desire?"

Reciter: _____ Story: _____

3.
> "Fool me once, shame on you,
> Fool me twice, shame on me."

Reciter: _____ Story: _____

4.
> "In His hand are the deep places of the earth."

Reciter: _____ Story: _____

5.
> "In the midnights of November
> When the dead man's fair is nigh,
> And the danger in the valley,
> And the anger in the sky."

Reciter: _____ Story: _____

6.
> "Is this the face that launched a thousand ships
> And burnt the topless towers of Ilium?"

Reciter: _____ Story: _____

7.

"Let me help."

Reciter: _____ Story: _____

8.

"That which we call a rose
By any other name would smell as sweet."

Reciter: _____ Story: _____

9.

"Suffering in torment and pain,
Laboring without end,
Dying and crying and
Lamenting over our burdens,
Only this way
Can we be happy."

Reciter: _____ Story: _____

10.

"My love has wings,
Slender, feathered things
With grace in upswept curve and tapered tip."

Reciter: _____ Story: _____

11.

"Tiger, tiger, burning bright
In the forests of the night."

Reciter: _____ Story: _____

12.

"Star light,
Star bright,
I wish I may,
I wish I might."

Reciter: _____ Story: _____

13.

"She walks in beauty like the night."

Reciter: _____ Story: _____

14.

"Perhaps we can't stroll to the music of the lute,
But must march to the sound of the drum."

Reciter: _____ Story: _____

15.

"Great Pan
Sounds the horn,
Marching time
To the rhyme
With his hoof,
With his hoof,
Forward, forward in our plan
We proceed as we began."

Reciter: _____ Story: _____

The Amazing Mr. Spock

Explain how Spock uses his logical mind to accomplish each
objective and name the story. (20 points)

1. He deciphers symbols on an obelisk. This enables him to enter
it, repair its asteroid deflector, and thus save a civilization from
extinction. _____
Story: _____

2. He discovers Scalosian hyperacceleration. _____
Story: _____

3. He negates Commodore Matt Decker's order to surrender command of the *Enterprise.* _____
Story: _____

4. He distinguishes between Garth as the mirror-Kirk and the real
Kirk and then shoots the mirror-Kirk with his phaser on stun.

_____

Story: _____

5. He saves McCoy from the fatal results of xenopolycthemia.

_____

Story: _____

6. He is able to lead Kirk to where the Vians are holding McCoy.

_____

Story: _____

7. He tracks down the cause of the Radiation Sickness which is plaguing all but one of the landing party who beamed down to Gamma Hydra IV. _____
Story: _____

8. He takes over control of the _Enterprise_ and locks her onto a forbidden course to Talos IV. _____
Story: _____

9. He figures that someone has tampered with the ship's computer to make it appear that Kirk is guilty of causing Ben Finney's death. _____ _____

_____

Story: _____

10. He tells Kirk of the course history will take if Edith Keeler lives or dies. _____

What They Think

Identify the speaker. (10 points)

_____ 1. "Pain is a thing of the mind. The mind can be controlled."

_____ 2. "Justice is the will of the stronger mind."

_____ 3. "Nothing ever changes except man."

_____ 4. "Believe me, Captain, immortality consists largely of boredom."

_____ 5. "The Good must transcend the Evil."

_____ 6. "What an idiotic way to travel! Spreading a person's molecules all over the universe!"

_____ 7. "All things have a point of origin."

_____ 8. "As you believe, so shall you do."

_____ 9. "Command and compassion is a fool's mixture."

_____ 10. "Courtesy is not for inferiors."

Do You Mind?

Spock's Vulcan mind can pick up the thoughts of others, fuse with the minds of others, influence the actions of others, and in certain cases, be totally unable to make contact State the result of the following endeavors. (15 points)

_____ 1. Kollos

_____ 2. Kirk, Scott, and McCoy at the O. K. Corral

_____ 3. The sleeping Kirk after his return from Holberg 917G

_____ 4. Kelinda

_____ 5. Gem

_____ 6. Gill

_____ 7. Lester/K

_____ 8. The guard on Eminiar VII

_____ 9. Sirah

_____ 10. Kirok

_____ 11. The horta

_____ 12. Nomad and the Other

_____ 13. McCoy

_____ 14. Dr. Van Gelder

_____ 15. The crew of the *Intrepid*

By the Book I

Match the person with the event, explain the event, and name the story. (30 points)

___	1. Komack	A.	Condition Green
___	2. Tracey	B.	Romulan Right of Statement
___	3. Finney	C.	Extraordinary Competency Hearing
___	4. Stocker	D.	Priority-1 Distress Call
___	5. Spock	E.	*Charges*: Galactic travel without a flight plan; absence of an identification beam; ignoring a starship's signal
___	6. Tongo Rad	F.	Evacuation Order
___	7. Mudd	G.	Violates the Prime Directive
___	8. Riley	H.	*Charges*: Piracy; violating flight regulations; entering hostile space
___	9. Baris	I.	Phase One Search
___	10. Proconsul Claudius Marcus	J.	Red Security Alert

By the Book II

Explain each directive and match it with the story in which it is applied. (20 points)

___ 1. "Dagger of the Mind" A. Prime Order of the Empire

___ 2. "The Man Trap" B. Missing Persons Procedures

___ 3. "A Taste of Armageddon" C. Medical Procedures Governing Scientific Teams

___ 4. "Let That Be Your Last Battlefield" D. Court-Martial Procedures

___ 5. "Mirror, Mirror" E. Destruct Sequence, Code 1

___ 6. "The Apple F. Weapons Rules Re: Penal Colonies

___ 7. "The Immunity Syndrome" G. Rescue Priority Order

___ 8. "The Menagerie" H. Consultation with the Advisory Service of the Federation Bureau of Industrialization

___ 9. "Bread and Circuses" I. General Order 24

___ 10. "The Cloud-Minders" J. Exploration Procedures

Ships

Name the Ship. (10 points)

1. Ship with which the *Enterprise* is to rendezvous to pick up vaccines earmarked for Theta VII. _____

2. First vessel to survey Star Sector 892, where Planet IV is located. _____

3. Survey ship which disappeared in the vicinity of the "forbidden planet." _____

4. Automated, old-style ore freighter deliberately destroyed by the M-5. _____

5. Balok's flagship of the First Federation. _____

6. Ship originally scheduled to transport the Karidian Players to Benecia. _____

7. Both ship and crew were the M-5's victims. _____

8. Ship which had been destroyed 100 years before the *Enterprise* arrived; yet the members of the Beta III landing were referred to by her name. _____

9. Kirk/L altered the *Enterprise's* plan to rendezvous with her. _____

10. She left *The Book.* _____

A. K. A.

Who is known by each of the following names? (15 points)

1. Baroner _____

2. Mr. Brack _____

3. Leo Francis Walsh _____

4. Beauregard _____

5. The "Pasteur of Archaeological Medicine" _____

6. The "Slum Area Angel" _____

7. "Bones" _____

8. "Nancy" _____

9. The "Last of the Barbarians" _____

10. The "Father of All Vulcans" _____

11. "Plum" _____

12. "The Others" _____

13. "Mr. Last of the Gods" _____

14. "Great Leader" _____

15. "Your Glory" _____

Romantic Interludes

Identify the beloved from the given initials and name the story.
(40 points)

1. Scott and M. R.
    Beloved _____ Story _____

2. Kirk and R. K.
    Beloved _____ Story _____

3. Spock and D.
    Beloved _____ Story _____

4. Arthur Coleman and J. L.
    Beloved _____ Story _____

5. Charles Evans and J. R.
    Beloved _____ Story _____

6. Gary Mitchell and E. D.
    Beloved _____ Story _____

7. Christine Chapel and R. K.
    Beloved _____ Story _____

8. Compton and M.
    Beloved _____ Story _____

9. Christopher Pike and V.
    Beloved _____ Story _____

10. McCoy and T. B.
    Beloved _____ Story _____

11. Kirk and A. S.
    Beloved _____ Story _____

12. The Romulan Commander and S.
    Beloved _____ Story _____

13. Kirk and D.
    Beloved _____ Story _____

14. Chekov and I. G.
    Beloved _____ Story _____

15. Kirk and O.
    Beloved _____ Story _____

16. Christine Chapel and S.
    Beloved _____ Story _____

17. Garth and M.
    Beloved _____ Story _____

18. Kirk and E.
    Beloved _____ Story _____

19. Spock and Z.
    Beloved _____ Story _____

20. Chekov and M. L.
    Beloved _____ Story _____

To Catch a Thief

Who stole each of the following? (10 points)

_____ 1. A shuttlecraft from Starbase 4

_____ 2. Watchmaker's tools

_____ 3. The *Aurora*

_____ 4. The Romulan Cloaking Device

_____ 5. The landing party's communicators on
Miri's Planet

_____ 6. The *Galileo II*

_____ 7. The main circulating pump from the
PXK reactor of the Pergium Production
Colony

_____ 8. Spock's brain

_____ 9. Dilithium crystals

_____10. 20th century clothes

Not to Be Believed

Each of the following is untrue. Why? (10 points)

1. At his competency trial, Kirk states twice that he took a landing party down to Gamma Hydra II.

2. Hodin informs Spock that Kirk never arrived on Gideon.

3. Kirk tells the Romulans that instrument failure caused a navigational error which inadvertently brought the *Enterprise* into Romulan space.

4. Spock informs Kirk that Major Christopher cannot be returned to Earth.

5. Kirk dies aboard a Romulan ship; in fact, his death is certified by a Romulan doctor.

6. Kirk jettisoned the *Enterprise* pod containing Records Officer Benjamin Finney before the red alert warning signal appeared on his viewing screen. This action resulted in Finney's death.

7. Scotty says he's 22 years old.

_____

8. Kirk identifies Khan's ship as a DY 500.

_____

9. Kirk, McCoy, and Spock believe that Septimus and his followers worship the Sun.

_____

10. Anan VII tells Kirk that the *Enterprise* has been destroyed by a tri-cobalt satellite explosion.

_____

How Distressing!

Distress calls always seem to cause distressing situations for some of the members of the *Enterprise*. Name the source of the call and the story. (20 points)

1. When the landing party arrives to treat his infected leg, they are made to grovel before him.
   Source _____ Story _____

2. They keep on sleeping right through their S.O.S.
   Source _____ Story _____

3. Wanted! Men Only!
   Source _____ Story _____

4. "S.O.S. Planet in Distress!"
   Source _____ Story _____

5. Priority A-1 call goes against the grain.
   Source _____ Story _____

6. A friendly "Hello" from miles below.
   Source _____ Story _____

7. After all these years, she finally figures out a way to get Kirk.
   Source _____ Story _____

8.   "Thanks for coming. You will surrender your ship to me."
      Source _____ Story _____

9.   They're really in *deep* trouble because of this thing.
      Source _____ Story _____

10.   Alien force sends two false signals to foster mutual hate
      and suspicion.
      Source _____ Story _____

Drink It In

Name the liquid refreshment and the story in which it is contained.
(20 points)

1. What McCoy is famous for "from here to Orion."
    Refreshment _____ Story _____

2. What Kirk was offered at Septimus' camp.
    Refreshment _____ Story _____

3. What Sulu would accept on Alfa 177 if the *Enterprise* was short of coffee.
    Refreshment _____ Story _____

4. What Chekov drank on Deep-Space Station K-7.
    Refreshment _____ Story _____

5. What Scott offered to Marvick as a wager.
    Refreshment _____ Story _____

6. What Spock accepted from Flint.
    Refreshment _____ Story _____

7. What Scott settled for in Tombstone.
    Refreshment _____ Story _____

8. What caused hyperacceleration.
Refreshment _____ Story _____

9. What Eminiar VII's favorite alcoholic beverage is called.
Refreshment _____ Story _____

10. What Balok offered his guests.
Refreshment _____ Story _____

Name Calling

Who was called each of the following, by whom, and in what
story? (30 points)

1. "Mr. Ears"
    The Called   The Caller   The Story

    _____   _____   _____

2. "Friendly Angel"
    The Called   The Caller   The Story

    _____   _____   _____

3. "The Executioner"
    The Called   The Caller   The Story

    _____   _____   _____

4. "Chairbound Paper-Pusher"
    The Called   The Caller   The Story

    _____   _____   _____

5. "Disease"
    The Called   The Caller   The Story

    _____   _____   _____

6. "Goodie Twoshoes"
    The Called   The Caller   The Story

    _____   _____   _____

7. "Judas-Goat"
   The Called   The Caller   The Story

   _____   _____   _____

8. "The Beast"
   The Called   The Caller   The Story

   _____   _____   _____

9. "Denebian Slime Devil"
   The Called   The Caller   The Story

   _____   _____   _____

10. "Mechanical Geisha"
    The Called   The Caller   The Story

    _____   _____   _____

The One and Only

Identify each of the following. (15 points)

_____ 1. Only survivor of its race at the present time.

_____ 2. Only one (No. 1) of its kind.

_____ 3. Only planet in our galaxy where the women are logical.

_____ 4. Only Earth grain which will grow on Sherman's Planet.

_____ 5. Only person aboard the *Enterprise* who can give orders to Kirk.

_____ 6. "Only love that money can buy."

_____ 7. Only one allowed to beam down to Gideon from the *Enterprise.*

_____ 8. Only survivor on Cestus III.

_____ 9. Only person ever to refuse a seat on the Federation Council.

_____ 10. Only survivor of the Talos IV crash.

_____ 11. Only person in the Mirror Universe
besides Kirk-2 who knows about the
Tantalus device.

_____ 12. Only thing it craves is salt.

_____ 13. Only human survivor of the Thasus crash.

_____ 14. Only reality here is death.

_____ 15. Only thing he claimed to have when he was
about to beam down to Triskelion was, like
Daniel, his faith.

"Expert-Tease"

Here are questions to test your "Trek-ability." You are not to refer back to any other part of this book. (77 points)

_____ 1. Who were the "Old Ones?"

_____ 2. How did Cochrane get the "perfect" mate?

_____ 3. Where does Charlie want the *Enterprise* to take him?

_____ 4. What planet were Kirk, Uhura, and Chekov supposed to land on when the Providers whisked them away to Triskelion?

_____ 5. Who is the member of the underground who escorts Kirk and Spock to Landru?

_____ 6. Who is the girl who tries to convince Sulu to join the "Space Hippies?"

_____ 7. Who is the crewman who requests and receives a Tribble from Uhura?

_____ 8. What is the name of the spy and pseudo-Andorian en route to Babel?

_____ 9. Who takes Sam's place on guard duty in the pergium mines and is subsequently killed by the horta?

_____ 10. What does the horta write?

_____ 11. Where did Magda Kovas grow up?

_____ 12. What is the name given to John Gill's last speech?

_____ 13. What is the name of the barber shop in the vicinity of Edith Keeler's 21st St. Mission?

_____ 14. What is the name of the 1930's movie star that neither Kirk nor McCoy had ever heard of?

_____ 15. In what paper does Edith Keeler's obituary appear?

_____ 16. What is going to be the topic of discussion at the Interplanetary Conference on Babel?

_____ 17. What is Chekov's full name?

_____ 18. What is the chief monetary unit of the United Federation of Planets?

_____ 19. Who pits Kirk against the captain of the Gorn ship?

_____ 20. What was the reason Spock advanced during Kirk's absence from the *Enterprise* when it leaves Starbase 11?

_____ 21. Who gives Angela Martine away as a bride?

_____ 22. What is the name of a Beta III informer?

_____ 23. Who has waited since the beginning of time
for a question?

_____ 24. What is the unit of exchange on Triskelion?

_____ 25. What does Kirk say to open the Obelisk on
Miramanee's Planet?

_____ 26. What is the Vulcan greeting?

_____ 27. What is Korob's "presto-change-o" device
called?

_____ 28. Who is Chekov's drill thrall on Triskelion?

_____ 29. What does the hysterical Dr. Harrison paint
on a bulkhead and inside one of the
Enterprise's elevators?

_____ 30. What does Uhura's name mean in Swahili?

_____ 31. What is the importance of the Fundamental
Declaration of the Martian Colonies?

_____ 32. What is the correct response to "Queen to
Queen's level three?"

_____ 33. Who records the proceedings at Scott's
murder trial?

_____ 34. How does Bele succeed in getting the *Enterprise* to go to Cheron?

_____ 35. What theory states that cultures develop in similar ways on similar planets?

_____ 36. What is Dr. Helen Noel's first suggestion to Kirk when he tests the neural potentiator?

_____ 37. What is the name of the ship that could have blown up because of Finney's carelessness?

_____ 38. What literary work was left behind by the Creators?

_____ 39. Who declares himself Organia's military governor?

_____ 40. What two products was Spock supposedly trading in on Organia?

_____ 41. What is the name of the card game Eve McHuron plays on Rigel XII?

_____ 42. What is given to Eve McHuron as a substitute for the Venus drug?

_____ 43. Where does Spock suggest that Lester/K be taken?

_____ 44. Why does Amanda slap Spock?

_____ 45. What is Harry Mudd's full name?

_____ 46. Why is Mudd convicted of fraud?

_____ 47. How often does the red bird come to Omega IV?

_____ 48. What is meant by a Class M planet?

_____ 49. Who defends Kirk at his court-martial trial?

_____ 50. Who doesn't respond to the nickname that Christine Chapel has always called him?

_____ 51. Who uses the code name Supervisor 194?

_____ 52. What is the name of the card game Kirk teaches the gangsters on Iotia?

_____ 53. What is the name of Dr. Sevrin's home planet?

_____ 54. What is the name of the alien space probe which merges with Nomad?

_____ 55. On what is each era of Sarpeidon history recorded?

_____ 56. What is the name of the device that programs the leader of the Eymorgs?

_____ 57. What infamous character inhabits the body of Hengist?

_____ 58. In what century do the *Star Trek* stories take place?

_____ 59. What finally makes Lt. Andrew Stiles overcome his prejudicial feelings against Spock?

_____ 60. What signals the presence of the Di-kironium Cloud Creature?

_____ 61. What does McCoy use to restore the horta?

_____ 62. Who is Kirk's favorite American President?

_____ 63. Who is the Kelvan Scotty gets drunk?

_____ 64. Which ruler was named after McCoy and Kirk?

_____ 65. Who became a bride and widow on the same day?

_____ 66. What kind of sounds are heard on Scalos?

_____ 67. What are Sylvia and Korob left to do?

_____ 68. What is the name of the portable device that records scientific data?

_____ 69. By what means is a starship controlled when its system fails to respond?

_____ 70. On what type of ranch did Ruth
                               Bonaventure grow up?

_____ 71. What does Kirk hear aboard the mock-up
                               Enterprise?

_____ 72. How is Mira Romaine's life saved?

_____ 73. Whom does Landru control?

_____ 74. What do the officials at Omaha Air Force
                               Base assume the *Enterprise* to be?

_____ 75. Who names the empath Gem?

_____ 76. What is the name of one of Gem's Vian
                               examiners?

_____ 77. What is the name of the Kelvans' home
                               galaxy?

Part II: Puzzles

Who Knows Where?

Find the names of places in the galaxy. Each entry is in a horizontal, vertical, or diagonal line, forwards or backwards. (49 points)

Antos	Fabrina	Orion	Zetar
Arcanis	Gideon	Platonius	
Ardana	Gorla	Rigel	
Beta	Halkan	Scalos	
Camus	Holberg	Signet	
Capella	Iotia	Space	
Cheron	Janus	Stars	
Daran	Kalanda	Sun	
Deneb	Kelva	Talos	
Dimorus	Marcos	Thasus	
Earth	Melkot	Tiburon	
Eden	Merak	Triacus	
Ekos	Minara	Triskelion	
Elas	Moon	Ursula	
Elba	Omega	Vulcan	
Exo	Organia	Zeon	

N	M	A	T	R	T	H	A	S	U	S	C	A	L	O	S
O	O	N	J	A	N	U	S	U	N	O	R	U	B	I	T
I	O	T	L	E	G	I	R	R	A	K	E	L	V	A	V
R	N	O	E	D	I	G	O	O	R	A	L	U	S	R	U
O	S	S	U	M	A	C	X	M	A	R	A	N	I	M	G
F	A	B	R	I	N	A	E	I	T	E	B	E	N	E	D
A	G	R	E	B	L	O	H	D	E	M	E	L	A	K	I
O	R	G	A	N	I	A	O	S	Z	S	O	C	R	A	M
S	S	O	K	E	G	P	S	U	I	N	O	T	A	L	P
R	T	L	B	E	T	A	O	E	Z	N	E	R	D	A	S
N	T	A	M	E	L	K	O	T	D	S	A	L	E	N	U
O	G	O	R	L	A	I	T	O	I	E	I	C	B	D	C
R	A	V	E	S	T	V	U	L	C	A	N	G	R	A	A
E	X	P	A	E	C	A	P	S	A	R	D	A	N	A	I
H	A	L	K	A	N	T	H	T	R	A	E	L	N	E	R
C	N	O	I	L	E	K	S	I	R	T	Z	E	O	N	T

The *Enterprise*

The following words are associated in some way with the *Enterprise*. Each entry is in a horizontal, vertical, or diagonal line, either forwards or backwards. (61 points)

aft	elevator	man	shuttlecraft
air	energize	matter	site
alarm	engine	orbit	space
alert	exit	pipe	tractor beam
band	fan	pod	train
base	Feinberger	power	transporter
bridge	flight	probe	tricorder
cabin	gun	radar	tubes
channel	helm	range	war (twice)
chapel	hold	review	warp
circuit	hull	risk	wire
clear	jet	roar	zone
data	lab	scan	
date	life support	sensor	
deck	log	shield	
duct	maiden run	ship	

```
D  U  C  T  F  A  R  C  E  L  T  T  U  H  S
E  N  E  R  G  I  Z  E  J  R  E  W  O  P  R
C  C  L  E  A  R  E  T  T  A  M  D  A  T  E
K  H  O  L  D  C  R  E  D  R  O  C  I  R  T
T  A  A  S  H  I  P  E  W  E  I  V  E  R
R  N  O  I  C  A  I  G  U  N  X  R  J  E  O
O  N  T  E  L  P  R  A  W  T  I  C  N  L  P
P  E  T  Z  E  E  N  A  C  S  T  U  B  E  S
P  L  R  O  B  L  A  B  K  E  R  I  W  V  N
U  M  A  N  L  A  E  E  S  N  B  T  F  A  A
S  H  I  E  L  D  N  G  E  F  A  N  D  T  R
E  E  N  R  U  A  G  D  N  Z  S  I  I  O  T
F  L  I  G  H  T  I  I  S  A  E  B  O  R  P
I  M  R  A  L  A  N  R  O  A  R  A  D  A  R
L  G  O  L  M  A  E  B  R  O  T  C  A  R  T
```

Role Playing

Actors and Characters List for Role Playing. (50 points)

Across

1. John Fiedler
5. Robert Walker, Jr.
7. Walter Koenig
9. Mariette Hartley
10. Lee Meriwether
12. Mark Lenard
14. Gary Lockwood
15. Harry Townes
18. Michael Dunn
19. Skip Homeier
20. Ricardo Montalban
21. George Takei
25. Kim Darby
27. Diana Muldaur
28. William Campbell
31. William Windom
32. Jane Wyatt
33. James Daly
34. Keye Luke
36. William Smithers
38. John Winston
40. Jeffrey Hunter
41. Sharon Acker
42. Grace Lee Whitney

Down

2. Daniel Brian
3. Robert Lansing
4. Nichelle Nichols
5. Glenn Corbett
6. William Marshall
8. Jill Ireland
10. Sandra Smith
11. Melvin Belli
13. Michael Strong
14. Sabrina Scharf
16. Warren Stevens
17. Sally Kellerman
19. Angelique Pettyjohn
20. James Doohan
22. Whit Bissel
23. Julie Newmar
24. France Nuyen
25. Roger C. Carmel
26. Elinor Donahue
27. DeForest Kelley
29. Bruce Hyde
30. Liam Sullivan
35. Leonard Nimoy
37. Michael Ansara
38. William Shatner
39. Michael Pollard

Characters

Alexander	Gorgan	Merik	Sarek
Amanda	Hedford	Miramanee	Scott
Charlie	Hengist	Miri	Seven
Chekov	Jahn	Mitchell	Sevrin
Cochrane	Kalomi	Mudd	Shahna
Cory	Kang	Mulhall	Singh
Daystrom	Kirk	Odona	Spock
Decker	Korby	Parmen	Sulu
Dehner	Kyle	Pike	Trelane
Elaan	Lester	Rand	Uhura
Eleen	Losira	Reger	Zarabeth
Flint	Lurry	Riley	
Gill	McCoy	Rojan	

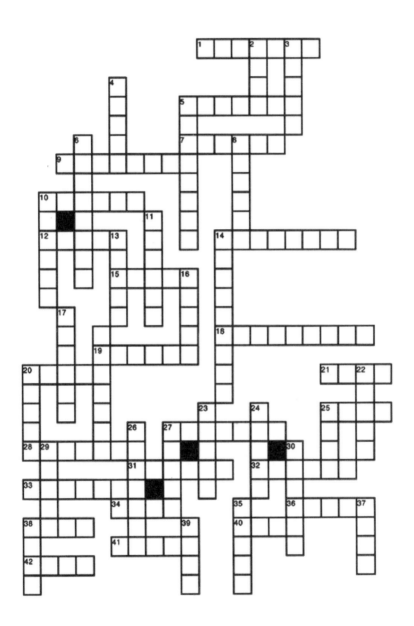

Part III: Answers

Answers to Ship-Shape

1.   NCC-1701
2.   James T. Kirk (T. is for Tiberius)
3.   Christopher Pike
4.   Lt. Commander Spock
5.   Lt. Commander Montgomery Scott ("Scotty")
6.   Lt. Commander Leonard McCoy ("Bones")
7.   Christine Chapel
8.   Walter Matthew Jeffries
9.   Lawrence Marvick
10.   Dr. Richard Daystrom
11.   50 billion credits
12. - 13.   Dilithium crystals and the matter/anti-matter integrator
14.   14.1
15. - 16.   The *Galileo* and the *Columbus*
17.   Stardate
18.   Exploration
19.   430
20.   The United Federation of Planets
21.   Sickbay
22.   Phasers
23.   The Herbarium
24.   Deck 8
25.   14

Your Score:

Answers to Well-Schooled

1.   Ensign Mallory's father

2.-3.   Tyree's Planet; Lieutenant

4.-5.   Capt. Garrovick; Lieutenant

6.-8.   The Vampire Cloud Creature; Garrovick's death;
        "Obsession"

9.   Ensign David Garrovick

10.-11. Ruth; Janice Lester

12.   Benjamin Finney

13.   Zefram Cochrane

14.   Garth

15.   Dr. Roger Korby

16.   John Gill

17.   Finnegan

18.   Matt Decker

19.   Robert Merik

20.   Commander Hanson

Your Score:

Answers to Mr. Spock

1. His sense of hearing
2. On his left side, near the back
3. T-negative; color: green
4. Copper
5. 242
6. Practically non-existent
7. Being slapped
8 His Vulcan inner eyelid
9. 250 years
10. Nurse Christine Chapel
11. They like Vulcans
12. The IDIC (Infinite Diversity in Infinite Combinations)
13. 4 years
14. A-7 Computer Expert
15. To become the Controller
16. Chinese
17. Gary Seven
18.-19. On Earth; 6 years
20. Apollo

Your Score:

Answers to What's My Line?

1. L
2. O
3. B
4. T
5. A
6. S
7. I
8. M
9. R
10. Y
11. D
12. N
13. W
14. P
15. V
16. E
17. K
18. H
19. U
20. F
21. X
22. C
23. J
24. G
25. Q

Your Score:

Answers to "Planet-Area"

1. Talos IV
2. The Amusement-Park Planet
3. Platonius
4. Sherman's Planet
5. Vendikar
6. Ardana
7. Deneb V
8. Gamma Trianguli VI
9. Berengaria VII
10. Elba II
11. Rigel XII
12. Pollux V
13. Organia
14. Omicron Ceti III
15. Gothos
16. Taurus II
17. Gideon
18. Triacus
19. Argelius II
20. Cheron

Your Score:

Answers to Planetary Authorities

1. Sarek
2. Ayelbourne
3. Plasus
4. Oxmyx
5. Parmen
6. Tharn
7. Anan VII
8. Kollos
9. Hodin
10. Nilz Baris
11. Gav (D)
12. Johnny Behan
13. Jaris
14. John Gill (D)
15. Petri
16. Nancy Hedford (D); then her body is used by "The Companion"
17. Akaar (D); Maab (D); Leonard James Akaar
18. Goro
19. Shras
20. Claudius Marcus
21. Bele

Your Score:

Answers to Clue Me In

See Appendix I for an alphabetical listing of the episodes.
See Appendix II for a chronological listing of the episodes by stardate.

1. "The Man Trap"
2. "Charlie X"
3. "Where No Man Has Gone Before"
4. "The Naked Time"
5. "The Enemy Within"
6. "Mudd's Women"
7. "What Are Little Girls Made Of?"
8. "Miri"
9. "Dagger of the Mind"
10. "The Corbomite Maneuver"
11. "The Menagerie"
12. "The Conscience of the King"
13. "Balance of Terror"
14. "Shore Leave"
15. "The *Galileo* Seven"
16. "The Squire of Gothos"
17. "Arena"
18. "Tomorrow Is Yesterday"
19. "Court-Martial"
20. "The Return of the Archons"
21. "Space Seed"
22. "A Taste of Armageddon"
23. "This Side of Paradise"
24. "The Devil in the Dark"
25. "Errand of Mercy"

26. "The Alternative Factor"
27. "The City on the Edge of Forever"
28. "Operation: Annihilate!"
29. "Amok Time"
30. "Who Mourns for Adonais?"
31. "The Changeling"
32. "Mirror, Mirror"
33. "The Apple"
34. "The Doomsday Machine"
35. "Catspaw"
36. "I, Mudd"
37. "Metamorphosis"
38. "Journey to Babel"
39. "Friday's Child"
40. "The Deadly Years"
41. "Obsession"
42. "Wolf in the Fold"
43. "The Trouble with Tribbles"
44. "The Gamesters of Triskelion"
45. "A Piece of the Action"
46. "The Immunity Syndrome"
47. "A Private Little War"
48. "Return to Tomorrow"
49. "Patterns of Force"
50. "By Any Other Name"
51. "The *Omega* Glory"
52. "The Ultimate Computer"
53. "Bread and Circuses"
54. "Assignment: Earth"
55. "Spock's Brain"

56. "The *Enterprise* Incident"
57. "The Paradise Syndrome"
58. "And the Children Shall Lead"
59. "Is There in Truth No Beauty?"
60. "Spectre of the Gun"
61. "Day of the Dove"
62. "For the World Is Hollow and I Have Touched the Sky"
63. "The Tholian Web"
64. "Plato's Stepchildren"
65. "Wink of an Eye"
66. "The Empath"
67. "Elaan of Troyius"
68. "Whom Gods Destroy"
69. "Let That Be Your Last Battlefield"
70. "The Mark of Gideon"
71. "That Which Survives"
72. "The Lights of Zetar"
73. "Requiem for Methusaleh"
74. "The Way to Eden"
75. "The Cloud-Minders"
76. "The Savage Curtain"
77. "All Our Yesterdays"
78. "Turnabout Intruder"

Your Score:

Answers to Where It Happened

1.   I

2.   G

3.   E

4.   C

5.   H

6.   A

7.   D

8.   J

9.   F

10. B

Your Score:

Answers to Travelogue

1. Ambassador Kollos in "Is There in Truth No Beauty?"
2. Dr. Simon Van Gelder in "Dagger of the Mind"
3. Alexander in "Plato's Stepchildren"
4. Zarabeth in "All Our Yesterdays"
5. Major John Christopher in "Tomorrow Is Yesterday"
6. Sam in "Charlie X"
7. Sargon in "Return to Tomorrow"
8. Krako in "A Piece of the Action"
9. Compton in "Wink of an Eye"
10. Gary Seven in "Assignment: Earth"

Your Score:

Answers to The Living End

1. Kirk and Garrovick land on Tycho IV with a matter/anti-matter time bomb. When the Vampire Cloud Creature smells their blood, it moves in for the kill, but Kirk and Garrovick manage to beam aboard the *Enterprise* seconds before the bomb detonates. "Obsession"

2. After the Creature kills Hengist, it leaves his body and wanders through the *Enterprise* searching for a new host. It soon returns and re-enters Hengist's body because everyone aboard has been so tranquilized that Kirk has "the happiest crew in space." Hengist is then tranquilized and his body is beamed into deep space at maximum dispersal in the hope that the Creature will have nothing to feed on and eventually die. "Wolf in the Fold"

3. The M-113 Creature, in the guise of Nancy Crater, is killed by McCoy as it attacks Kirk. As it is dying, McCoy sees the Creature in its true form. "The Man Trap"

4. Vaal is first weakened when Kirk prevents the Vaalians from feeding it. He then orders the total phaser power of the ship to be concentrated on Vaal, which results in the machine god's destruction. "The Apple"

5. Kirk pilots the *Constellation*, which is all set to explode, right down the throat of the berserker. He is then beamed aboard the *Enterprise* just as the *Constellation* is to blow up. "The Doomsday Machine"

6. Nomad destroys itself because Kirk confronts it with this logical sequence:
   a) It mistook Kirk for its inventor, Roykirk.
   b) It didn't correct its mistake.
   c) A mistake is an imperfection which, as Nomad says, must be corrected by sterilization. "The Changeling"

7. Kirk destroys the Amoeba-like Organism with a timed anti-matter charge directed at the chromosome coordinator in its nucleus. This was in accordance with the information Spock relayed from his shuttlecraft probe. "The Immunity Syndrome"

8. McCoy discovers that ultraviolet light will kill the Creatures and not harm humans. Kirk then orders ultraviolet satellite flares to be set off over Deneva. "Operation: Annihilate!"

9. Led by Kirk and Kang, the Terrans and the Klingons stop their warfare and pretend to be friends. Together they succeed in laughing the dwindling Entity that feeds on hate off the *Enterprise* and into space. "Day of the Dove"

10. Kirk gets the M5 to admit it has committed murder. It then relinquishes control of the *Enterprise*, leaving the ship defenseless, and proceeds to have a nervous breakdown as it speaks its final words: "This unit must die." "The Ultimate Computer"

Your Score:

Answers to In Command

1. D

2. H

3. E

4. J

5. I

6. B

7. C

8. F

9. A

10. G

Your Score:

Answers to An Unusual Kiss

1. Shahna is Kirk's drill thrall on the planet Triskelion. After he kisses her, he knocks her out so that he can escape from his detention cell. "The Gamesters of Triskelion"

2. As part of the evening's entertainment, Parmen causes Uhura and Christine Chapel to be brought down from the *Enterprise* as partners for Kirk and Spock. Through mind control he forces both couples to embrace against their will. "Plato's Stepchildren"

3. Although it seems that Kirk and Mulhall are embracing, they have really lent their bodies to Sargon and his wife Thalassa for one last physical expression of love before they return to their non-corporeal existence. "Return to Tomorrow"

4. Andrea is an android created by Dr. Roger Korby. Just as Korby had previously done with Andrea, Kirk orders Andrea to kiss him. Immediately after the kiss, she tries to slap Kirk as Korby has programmed her to do, but Kirk passionately kisses her instead. Totally confused by this new emotional sensation, Andrea leaves the room. Then she meets the android Kirk and tries to kiss him. When she is repelled, she destroys him. Next, she approaches Korby and as she comes in close for a kiss, her phaser discharges, killing them both. "What Are Little Girls Made Of?"

5. The Caretaker provides Kirk with a romantic diversion by conjuring up Ruth, one of the Captain's love interests 15 years earlier. "Shore Leave"

6. This kiss is a false image which Dr. Tristan Adams planted in Kirk's mind in conjunction with the neural potentiator treatment. The event supposedly occurred on the night when Kirk "fell in love" with Dr. Helen Noel at the Science Laboratory's Christmas party. Needless to say, in the current situation, Helen is most uncomfortable with Kirk's programmed protestations of affection. "Dagger of the Mind"

7. When Kirk kisses Lenore Karidian, the 19-year-old daughter of the man believed to be Kodos the Executioner, he little suspects that Lenore is a murderer herself. "Conscience of the King"

8. A victim of amnesia, Kirk, known to the natives as Kirok, falls in love with Miramanee, the chief's daughter. Their first kiss leads to the altar and Kirk's only marriage in the series. "The Paradise Syndrome"

9. After a bitter fight which culminates in tears and a confession that she thinks everyone hates her, Elaan's behavior moves Kirk to wipe those tears from her stained cheeks. In so doing, he exposes himself to a bio-chemical substance which is present in all Elasian women's tears. It acts as a love potion which no man can resist, a potion that has no antidote (until McCoy's untested discovery). Inevitably, however, Kirk's ultimate antidote proves to be the *Enterprise*. "Elaan of Troyius"

10. Kirk turns on all his manly charms in order to extract information from Sylvia, a beautiful woman who is really an alien creature. In fact, in Kirk's arms she assumes the appearance of

many beautiful women. Unable to cope with her new feminine sensations, Sylvia reveals many secrets. Kirk pushes her away and admits he has used her in the same way she had planned to use him. Sylvia then orders Kirk back to his cell. "Catspaw"

11. Sylvia is Billy Claiborne's girl. She works in a saloon and when Kirk, Spock, McCoy, Scott, and Chekov come in and order drinks, she, like everyone else in Tombstone, sees them as the Clanton gang. To Chekov's surprise and obvious delight, she recognizes him as Billy Claiborne and greets him with a great big kiss. "Spectre of the Gun"

12. Spock and McCoy try to follow Kirk out of the Library, but inadvertently step back in time 100,000 years into a barren, icy world, whose sole human inhabitant is Zarabeth. Spock begins regressing back to the primitive state of the early Vulcans— irrational and passionate. He eats animal flesh and likes it; he exhibits real hostility towards McCoy; and he enjoys the sensations of feeling attracted to Zarabeth and kissing her. Because Spock and McCoy haven't been properly "prepared" by the Atavachron for life in this world, they will die unless they return to the present, but Zarabeth can't join them because she had been "prepared" to live only where she is. And so, the lovers part. "All Our Yesterdays"

13. Leila Kalomi is a botanist with the Sandoval Colony on Omicron Ceti III. Six years earlier she knew and loved Spock on Earth, although her love was never reciprocated. On seeing her again, Spock is his usual stiff self until she shows him where she discovered some rather unique spores, and he comes

under their effect. Freed now from all his inhibitions, he gives expression to his romantic feelings. He kisses her and when Kirk calls him back to duty, ignores him. Spock would be more than content to remain on this planet for the rest of his life, but the Captain has other ideas. "This Side of Paradise"

14. Lt. Marla McGivers, Controls System Specialist and Historian, whose area of concentration is late 20th century Earth events, falls in love with Khan Noonien Singh, a 20th-century military tyrant who, after two centuries in space, is awakened with a number of his genetically advanced crew from a state of suspended animation. After Khan sweeps Marla into his arms, kisses her, and boasts of his plans for power, she agrees to help him and his followers take control of the *Enterprise*. Their efforts eventually fail and rather than face a court-martial, Marla decides to be exiled with Khan to a primitive planet. "Space Seed"

15. Old age and death do not exist on Gamma Trianguli VI and, therefore, there is no need for "replacements" because Vaal, a computerized god that the natives feed and worship, guarantees immortality. When Makora and Sayana kiss, an idea they get from watching Chekov and Yeoman Martha Landon embrace, they are told by their leader Akuta that such conduct is an act of disobedience to Vaal. Vaal feels threatened by the visitors from the *Enterprise* and teaches the natives how to kill. Kirk and crew destroy Vaal, and the natives must now engage in the conventional cycles of life. Obviously, Makora and Sayana have a head start. "The Apple"

Your Score:

Answers to Firsts

1. Black Star
2. The *Enterprise*
3. - 4. Kirk; Uhura
5. - 6. Miramanee; Kirk
7. Number One
8. Tom Nellis
9. "Where No Man Has Gone Before"
10. Where to look for Kirk, Uhura, and Chekov
11. Spock
12. "The *Galileo* Seven"
13. Uhura
14. Kirk
15. McCoy
16. Alpha Centauri
17. 2018
18. Sarek
19. Mudd
20. Omicron Ceti III
21. Gamma Hydra IV
22. Transport
23. Leila Kalomi
24. Latimer
25. That Lt. Mira Romaine could return to duty

Your Score:

Answers to Numbered Places

1. Ensign David Garrovick's room and the place of entry for the Vampire Cloud Creature.

2. Place where Lester/K is held in isolation with round-the-clock security.

3. Base on Talos IV which the Talosians conjure up for Pike and his landing party to see, including the expedition's leader, Dr. Theodore Haskins

4. Number of Dr. Leonard McCoy's room aboard the *Enterprise*.

5. Yeoman Janice Rand's room on Deck 12 of the *Enterprise*.

6. Gary Seven's apartment in which the Beta 5 computer is housed and where Roberta Lincoln works.

7. Last reported position of the *Intrepid*.

8. Room which Kirk and Spock share in the rooming house where Edith Keeler lives.

9. Destination of the child survivors of Triacus.

10. Place where the tape recording of the dialogue between Black Jack and Blue Jay about the *Enterprise* is kept.

Your Score:

Answers to Disease-O-Mania

1. "The Deadly Years"

2. "Operation: Annihilate!"

3. "Metamorphosis"

4. "The Mark of Gideon"

5. "The Way to Eden"

6. "The City on the Edge of Forever"

7. "This Side of Paradise"

8. "The Naked Time"

9. "And the Children Shall Lead"

10. "Turnabout Intruder"

Your Score:

Answers to I, My, Mine

1. F. "Who Mourns for Adonais?"

2. E. "Whom Gods Destroy"

3. J. "Charlie X"

4. B. "What Are Little Girls Made Of?"

5. I. "Space Seed"

6. A. "Where No Man Has Gone Before"

7. D. "Dagger of the Mind"

8. H. "The Squire of Gothos"

9. G. "I, Mudd" or "Mudd's Women"

10. C. "Bread and Circuses"

Your Score:

Answers to Food for Thought

1. Kaferian apples in "Where No Man Has Gone Before."

2. Celery in "The Man Trap."

3. Haggis in "The Savage Curtain."

4. Plomeek soup in "Amok Time."

5. Turkey in "Charlie X."

6. Grapes in "Plato's Stepchildren."

7. The egg in "The Way to Eden."

8. Ice cream in "The Naked Time."

9. Chicken soup in "Tomorrow Is Yesterday."

10. Dietary salad in "The Corbomite Maneuver."

Your Score:

Answers to A Place in Space

1. Regulus V

2. Typerias

3. Mudd's Planet

4. Dimorus

5. Minara II

6. Sigma Draconis VI

7. Excalbia

8. Ursula

9. Maynark IV

10. Memory Alpha

Your Score:

Answers to Bossism

1. Therapist for Dr. Adams

2. Secretary to Agents 201 and 347

3. Administrative Assistant to Commodore Mendez

4. Kohm military leader for Capt. Tracey

5. Slave of Proconsul Claudius Marcus

6. One of Galt's drill thralls, who is assigned to Uhura by the Providers

7. One of Col. Travis' security guards

8. Assistant to Nilz Baris

9. One of Bela Oxmyx's gangsters

10. Court Buffoon for all the Platonians

Your Score:

Answers to Once Upon a Time

1. Zefram Cochrane looks like a man in his mid-thirties. When Kirk learns that he is the same Zefram Cochrane whose theories on space travel he had to study at the Academy, he is astonished to find him still alive. Cochrane explains that since the time he and his disabled ship were rescued 150 years ago, when he was 87, he has constantly been rejuvenated by "The Companion."

2. The Atavachron is a time machine which allows its user to step back into any past time period. This device is located in the Library on the planet Sarpeidon and is operated by Mr. Atoz, whose job it is to prepare the body of its user for life in the past.

3. Yarnek is a rock creature on the planet Excalbia. He has never encountered Earthlings before and decides to arrange a contest between Good and Evil to study the reactions of the opposing forces. For this purpose Yarnek brings characters out of the past to life again. He allies Kirk and Spock with Abraham Lincoln and Surak against the evil powers of Genghis Khan, Col. Green, Zora, and Kahless.

4. The Guardian of Forever is a time portal through which a paranoic McCoy jumps. Kirk and Spock go after him and all three are eventually reunited in New York City in the year 1930.

5. The *Enterprise's* collision with a black star sent her traveling back in time to the year 1960 where the ship was picked up on radar on the planet Earth and called a UFO.

6. *The Book* was left on Iotia by the crew of the *Horizon* 100 years earlier. It contains a history of Chicago mobs of the 1920's and is the blueprint for Iotian society.

7. John Gill was sent to Ekos as a cultural ambassador; instead, he patterned Ekosian society on the Nazi movement of the 1930's and wound up as the Ekosians' figurehead Führer.

8. It is believed that the Preservers took races that faced extinction on Earth and scattered them throughout the galaxy. This theory explains why so many planetary inhabitants speak English.

9. The Dim Time is that period in the history of Gamma Trianguli VI when Akuta received his antennae. It is so far back that he barely remembers it. The inhabitants' way of life hasn't changed since then either; that is, until the *Enterprise* arrives.

10. The Empire TV network on Planet 892-IV presents gladiatorial contests and executions in the style of ancient Rome.

Your Score:

Answers to It Ain't Necessarily So

1. This is not the real *Enterprise*, only a mock-up created by the authorities on Gideon. "The Mark of Gideon"

2. Appearances are indeed deceiving. Eden's fruit is deadly and the plant life is full of acid. "The Way to Eden"

3. When Kirk and the landing party try to get out of town, they can't because the Melkotians have placed a force field around the area. "Spectre of the Gun"

4. Life really does exist on Scalos, but as a result of radiation released in volcanic eruptions, the remaining Scalosians have been hyperaccelerated. They move so fast in time that even when they talk, their voices can only be heard as whining mosquito sounds. "Wink of an Eye"

5. Kirk and his landing party unfortunately find out this "paradise" contains plants which throw poisonous thorns and rocks which explode on contact. "The Apple"

6. Omicron Ceti III is a static world in which everyone is infected by spores which make the inhabitants totally non-productive. "This Side of Paradise"

7. Yonada is really a spaceship headed on a collision course with Daran V. "For the World Is Hollow and I Have Touched the Sky"

8. Spock is not the Spock we know. His body is present, but his brain is missing. It was stolen from his body when he was aboard the *Enterprise*. "Spock's Brain"

9. The computer was tampered with by the man whose death Kirk is supposed to have caused; therefore, the sequence of events was altered. "Court-Martial"

10. This grain has been poisoned. When the Tribbles eat it, it turns into inert matter which cannot be absorbed by the animals' digestive systems. "The Trouble with Tribbles"

Your Score:

Answers to Sons and Daughters

1. Spock

2. Tongo Rad

3. Shaun Geoffrey

4. Leonard James

5. Jamie

6. David

7. Miramanee

8. Odona

9. Lenore

10. Peter

11. Don

12. Droxine

13. Tula

14. Tommy

15. Kara

Your Score:

Answers to Is That Really You?

1. Isis seems to be a black Siamese cat until she momentarily reveals herself as an exceedingly beautiful woman. "Assignment: Earth"

2. It seems that after five years, Christine Chapel's fiancé has at last been found. In reality, the man to whom Christine was engaged no longer exists, for all that is left of Roger is his brain, which is now housed in an android body. "What Are Little Girls Made Of?"

3. Vina seems to be a beautiful young woman. Actually, Vina is a deformed middle-aged woman whom the Talosians restored as best they could after they found her bruised and broken body. Unfortunately, they had no human model to follow in putting her back together, but they compensated for this by giving Vina and all who behold her the illusion of a beautiful young woman. "The Menagerie"

4. Kirk's old friend greets him at his arrival on Elba II. Actually, the real Dr. Cory has been tricked by Garth (who has changed himself into Cory) and it is he who welcomes Kirk. "Whom Gods Destroy"

5. The Organians appear to be simple people who are totally unconcerned about Kirk's insistence that they allow the Federation to protect them from the Klingons. In reality, the Organians do not have bodies, but are incorporeal creatures of pure thought who have merely assumed humanoid form to show both the Federation and the Klingons that they can prevent these two warring factions from fighting each other. "Errand of Mercy"

6. To McCoy, Nancy Crater is just as he remembers her, but the real Nancy has been dead for more than a year. The M-113 Creature killed Nancy for her body salts and "It" is now living as Nancy with Dr. Crater because he keeps "It" supplied with salt tablets. "The Man Trap"

7. Balok appears on the *Enterprise* screen as a foreboding giant. He is actually a friendly dwarf who is merely hiding behind the image he projects. "The Corbomite Maneuver"

8. Flint seems to be immortal, according to his own claim of having lived as many different people for more than 6,000 years. According to McCoy's medical findings, however, Flint is actually aging and will eventually die a natural death because the process of tissue regeneration and biological renewal has ceased since he left Earth's atmosphere. "Requiem for Methusaleh"

9. Losira appears to be a beautiful young woman, but each Losira we see is actually a replica of a long-dead Kalandan of that name and is a projection of such great intensity that the mere touch of her hand causes cellular disruption in her victim. "That Which Survives"

10. Karidian passes himself off as the director and featured actor of a traveling theater company, The Karidian Players. In reality, he is Kodos, a former governor of Tarsus IV who, twenty years earlier, arbitrarily sentenced the "inferior" half of that planet's population to death because of a food shortage. "The Conscience of the King"

Your Score:

Answers to Personal Attacks

1. Elaan in "Elaan of Troyius"

2. Janice Rand in "The Enemy Within"

3. Charlie Evans in "Charlie X"

4. Thalassa in "Return to Tomorrow"

5. Lawrence Marvick in "Is There in Truth No Beauty?"

6. Apollo in "Who Mourns for Adonais?"

7. Salish in "The Paradise Syndrome"

8. Scotty in "The Trouble with Tribbles"

9. Lenore Karidian in "The Conscience of the King"

10. Thelev in "Journey to Babel"

Your Score:

Answers to Officialdom

1. He tried to make Kirk abandon the search for the *Galileo*. "The *Galileo* Seven"

2. He overrode Kirk's wishes to comply with Code 710 and insisted that Kirk beam down with him to Eminiar VII. "A Taste of Armageddon"

3. He wouldn't allow the *Enterprise* to divert to Vulcan and ordered Kirk to proceed at once to Altair VI. "Amok Time"

4. After calling an Extraordinary Competency Hearing to determine Kirk's fitness for command, he took over command of the *Enterprise*. "The Deadly Years"

5. He denied Kirk permission to stay on a parallel course with Yonada. "For the World Is Hollow and I Have Touched the Sky"

Your Score:

Answers to Of Therapeutic Value?

1.   Benjasidrine

2.   Theragen

3.   Cordrazine

4.   Cyalodin

5.   Sodium Chloride (Salt)

6.   Tri-Ox Compound

7.   Ronoxiline D

8.   The Venus Drug

9. - 10. Coralin and a Vitalizer B Pressure Packet

11.   Formazine

12.   Stokaline

13.   Celebium (resulting in radiation poisoning)

14.   Spores

15.   Masaform D

Your Score:

Answers to The Other Kirk

1. "Spectre of the Gun" Everyone in town thinks Kirk is Ike Clanton, the leader of the Clanton gang. The Melkots have arranged this scenario because the *Enterprise* violated their sector of space.

2. "Whom Gods Destroy" Garth learned the technique of cellular metamorphosis on Antos IV. This gives him the ability to look like anyone he chooses. Here he changes his appearance to look like Kirk in order to deceive Spock, who has come to rescue the Captain.

3. "The Enemy Within" Because of contamination from some magnetic ore brought up from the surface of Alfa 177, the transporter malfunctions and splits Kirk into two beings: one, good but weak-willed; the other, evil and strong-willed.

4. "The Paradise Syndrome" After accidentally gaining entrance to the inside of an obelisk and falling down a flight of stairs, Kirk suffers amnesia.

5. "Plato's Stepchildren" Parmen, the philosopher-king of Platonius, wants McCoy to remain on his planet. He figures that McCoy will agree rather than see his Captain suffer. Parmen humbles both Kirk and Spock and makes them objects of ridicule by forcing them to respond the way he wants.

6. "Mirror, Mirror" An ion storm momentarily causes a transporter malfunction as Kirk and his landing party are beaming up from Halkan. Instead of materializing on the *U. S. S.*

Enterprise, they find themselves in an alternative universe aboard the *I. S. S. Enterprise* while, at the same time, an evil Kirk and his landing party materialize aboard the *U. S. S. Enterprise*.

7. "Turnabout Intruder" Dr. Janice Lester uses the life/entity transfer machine she has discovered on Camus II to switch personalities with Kirk. She emerges as the Captain and he, in turn, is trapped inside Janice Lester's body.

8. "What Are Little Girls Made Of?" Dr. Roger Korby has his creation of an android Kirk beam up to the *Enterprise* from Exo III. While the android was being made, Kirk kept repeating the words, "Mind your own business, Mr. Spock! I'm sick of your halfbreed interference! Do you hear?" When the android Kirk says these words to Spock, Spock realizes that an android is speaking and that the real Kirk is in trouble.

9. "Return to Tomorrow" Kirk allows Sargon to borrow his body so that Sargon can build an android body for himself. In the meantime, Kirk's intellect is housed in a globe.

10. "The *Enterprise* Incident" Kirk is on a mission to steal the Romulan Cloaking Device. After allowing himself to be captured and declared "dead" aboard the Romulan ship, Kirk's body is returned to the *Enterprise*. He is speedily "restored to life" and undergoes surgery to look like a Romulan. This includes altering his ears. He returns to the Romulan vessel, successfully completes his mission, and returns again to the operating table.

Your Score:

Answers to Animal, Vegetable, Mineral

1. A mugato

2. A creeper

3. A doglike creature

4. A borgia plant

5. A mako root

6. An Arcturian dog-bird

7. Spican flame gems

8. Quadrotriticale

9. A black Siamese cat

10. Sahsheer

Your Score:

Answers to Weaponry

1. Neural Potentiator

2. Tantalus Field

3. Illogic

4. Mortae

5. Servo

6. Instrument of Obedience

7. Ultrasonics, Hypersonics, or Sound

8. Kligat

9. Lirpa

10. A tranquilizing gas grenade

Your Score:

Answers to In Other Words

1.   E
2.   G
3.   J
4.   H
5.   D
6.   C
7.   I
8.   F
9.   A
10.   B

Your Score:

Answers to Mineral Deposits

1. Used to control certain bacterial plagues, zienite gas caused mental retardation in the Troglytes; Ardana; "The Cloud-Minders."

2. Only known cure for Rigellian fever; Holberg 917G; "Requiem for Methusaleh."

3. A psychokinetic-producing drug; Platonius; "Plato's Stepchildren."

4. An energy metal which is used in nuclear reactors; Janus VI; "The Devil in the Dark."

5. Needed to maintain life-support systems on planetoid colonies; Capella VI; "Friday's Child."

Your Score:

Answers to To the Death

1. Garth sends her out into Elba II's poisonous atmosphere, but before she chokes to death, he detonates an explosive crystal which he had placed in her necklace. "Whom Gods Destroy"

2. They die in an automobile accident. "Assignment: Earth"

3. Kryton breaks his neck. "Elaan of Troyius"

4. The M5 kills him. "The Ultimate Computer"

5. He dies fighting the Gorns. "Arena"

6. Tracey shoots him to death. "The *Omega* Glory"

7. He dies of cellular disruption caused by Losira's touch. "That Which Survives"

8. He dies aboard the *Enterprise* from escaping coolant fluid. "Balance of Terror"

9. Keel kills him with a klugat. "Friday's Child"

10. He poisons himself with cyalodin. "And the Children Shall Lead"

11. Melakon machine-guns him to death. "Patterns of Force"

12. She dies of a brain hemorrhage caused by the Zetarians when they invade her body. "The Lights of Zetar"

13. With Charlie's help, his ship blows up. "Charlie X"

14. Ruk pushes him off a precipice. "What Are Little Girls Made Of?"

15. He steps on a rock which immediately explodes. "The Apple"

16. He dies of loneliness "at the hands" of the neural potentiator. "Dagger of the Mind"

17. He is strangled by tubing which Mitchell wills to encase his neck. "Where No Man Has Gone Before"

18. He dies on a suicide mission into the heart of the Doomsday Machine. "The Doomsday Machine"

19. Gladiator Claudius Marcus kills him with a sword. "Bread and Circuses"

20. She is run over by a car. "The City on the Edge of Forever"

21. Lenore Karidian stabs him to death. "The Conscience of the King"

22. She dies from the heat of Kirk's phaser (even though it's set on stun) because of the deadly virus at work within her. "Miri"

23. He dies of insanity because he could not live with what he saw after looking at Kollos. "Is There in Truth No Beauty?"

24. He eats poisonous fruit on Eden. "The Way to Eden"

25. Rojan reduces her into a block, which he then crumbles into minute particles with his hand. "By Any Other Name"

Your Score:

Answers to Matrimonial Alliances

1. Eleen
2. Magda Kovas
3. Eve McHuron
4. Nancy
5. Ruth Bonaventure
6. Sybo
7. Elaine
8. Mara
9. Aurelan
10. Miramanee
11. Martha
12. Natira
13. Stella
14. Philana
15. Lydia
16. Amanda
17. Thalassa
18. T'Pring
19. Nona
20. Janet

Your Score:

Answers to Superlatives

1. A Tribble

2. Apollo

3. Edith Keeler

4. Surak

5. The existence of Platonius

6. To arm Tyree and his Hillpeople in order to preserve a balance of power between them and the Klingon-armed Villagers

7. Rodinium

8. The Dohlman

9. Charlie (Charles Evans)

10. The removal of Spock's brain

11. Bang! Bang!

12. The cloud-city of Stratos

13. Garth

14. As Captain of the *Galileo*

15. The horta

Your Score:

Answers to Thought Manifestations

1. McCoy*

2. Rodriguez*

3. Apollo for Carolyn Palamas

4. Tonia Barrows*

5. The Talosians. This is where Pike first saw Vina.

6. Yarnek dug into Kirk's mind and came up with one of Kirk's heroes.

7. Trelane, so that he could duel with Kirk.

8. Sulu*

9. The Talosians put in Tango, Pike's horse, as part of a picture scene.

10. Mitchell conjured up his own "Garden of Eden" on Delta Vega.

*These were all made of multi-cellular castings which the Caretaker of the Amusement Planet provided from his visitors' thoughts.

Your Score:

Answers to Gifts

1. His unborn child.
2. An 18th century French dress, long gloves, and a high hair-do.
3. A wedding dress, wedding slippers, and royal jewels.
4. A filter mask.
5. Her jewelled dagger.
6. A necklace with a diamond pendulum containing a drop of a powerful explosive which he had invented.
7. A kithara (Greek lyre).
8. A shield carried by Pericles.
9. A scroll of ancient Greek cures written by Hippocrates.
10. A pink rosebud; perfume.

Your Score:

Answers to Kirkathon

1. Mudd in "I, Mudd"

2. Nomad in "The Changeling"

3. The "Space Hippies" in "The Way to Eden"

4. Miri in "Miri"

5. Commodore Wesley in "The Ultimate Computer"

6. Tyree in "A Private Little War"

7. Miramanee in "The Paradise Syndrome"

8. Lenore Karidian in "The Conscience of the King"

9. Finnegan in "Shore Leave" and Spock in "This Side of Paradise"

10. The androids in "I, Mudd"

Your Score:

Answers to Ceremonial Occasions

1. The music was taped.

2. "I give you my heart and my possessions."

3. Heir Apparent

4. Sacrilege

5. Kah-if-farr

6. Kal-if-fee

7. Koon-ut-kal-if-fee

8. A ceremony in which two men become brothers.

9. Kirk and Tyree

10. The right hand is raised with a separation between the third and fourth fingers; sometimes the first and second fingers are touched to another's.

Your Score:

Answers to Assorted Quotes

1. Cloud William
2. Sulu to Rand
3. Odona
4. Adam about Kirk
5. Surak to Kirk
6. Kang
7. Nona about Kirk and herself
8. Spock to Stonn about T'Pring
9. Spock to Scott
10. Kirk

Your Score:

Answers to Life Savers

1. Dr. Miranda Jones is persuaded to enter into a Vulcan mind meld with Spock so that his sanity may be restored. "Is There in Truth No Beauty?"

2. Kirk convinces the Vians that they should exercise what Gem has just learned: compassion. "The Empath"

3. Lt. Marla McGivers frees him. "Space Seed"

4. In a last minute act of desperation, Spock jettisons the fuel and ignites it. The *Enterprise* spots the flare and beams the crew aboard just as the *Galileo* disintegrates. "The *Galileo* Seven"

5. McCoy, who fears the worst, is given permission to administer a Tri-Ox compound to Kirk to compensate for Vulcan's thin air. Instead, he injects a drug which simulates death. When Kirk collapses as he and Spock are fighting, McCoy accuses Spock of killing the Captain. He then has Kirk's body beamed aboard the *Enterprise*. "Amok Time"

6. Wesley gambles that the *Enterprise* is completely helpless and not merely playing dead. He holds fire. "The Ultimate Computer"

7. Spock asks McCoy to give him an experimental drug to increase his blood supply in order to enable him to give his father a transfusion. McCoy successfully administers the drug to both Spock and Sarek. Sarek then undergoes and survives the operation. "Journey to Babel"

8. McCoy uses intense light to destroy all the flying parasites on the planet. "Operation: Annihilate!"

9. McCoy tells his fellow officers to return to the *Enterprise* without him, for he cannot leave anyone in need. He then ministers to Spock-2, who quickly revives and escorts the group to the *I. S. S. Enterprise's* Transporter Room, thereby ensuring their safe return. "Mirror, Mirror"

10. Trelane's parents appear as globes of light, reprimand their son, apologize to Kirk, and free him from the prison Trelane has created. They make Trelane leave with them, still scolding him for his actions as Trelane protests that they always spoil his fun. "The Squire of Gothos"

Your Score:

Answers to Triangles

1. Stonn wins T'Pring, just as T'Pring planned.

2. Carolyn is attracted to Apollo but gives him up in the line of duty.

3. Neither gets Kirk: Miri is too young and Janice Rand is too much in awe of him ever to think that he could really be interested in her.

4. In assuming human forms, Rojan and Kelinda acquire human emotions and, as Kirk foresaw, returning to Kelva is no longer in their future plans.

5. Out of jealousy, Marvick tries to kill Kollos but dies as a result.

6. Billy Claiborne (alias Chekov) is shot down by Morgan Earp, but since history really didn't happen that way, we assume that Claiborne got the girl.

7. Neither Flint nor Kirk win Reena; she's incapable of handling conflicting human emotions and "dies."

8. Rael and Deela remain on Scalos. Kirk simply can't keep up with them!

9. Both Spock and McCoy return to their own world and Zarabeth remains in hers.

10. Kirk gallantly defends Teresa from Trelane's advances by making Trelane so angry that he turns his attention away from Teresa and on to himself.

Your Score:

Answers to Notables

1. Leader of the Feeders of Vaal on Gamma Trianguli VI.
2. Chief Processing Engineer of the Pergium Production Colony on Janus VI.
3. Chief Librarian on Sarpeidon.
4. Head Miner on Rigel XII.
5. Leader of the Yangs on Omega IV.
6. Archaeologist on Planet M-113.
7. Governor of an insane asylum on Elba II.
8. Launch Director at McKinley Rocket Base, Planet Earth.
9. Master Thrall on Triskelion.
10. Computer Center Chief on Starbase 11.
11. Leader of the "Onlies" on Miri's Planet.
12. Botanist on Omicron Ceti III.
13. "Leader" of the Eymorgs on Sigma Draconis VI.
14. Missionary on Earth.
15. Research Biologist on Deneva.
16. Boss of the Southside Territory on Iotia.
17. Commander of the Kalandan Outpost Planet.
18. Manager of Deep-Space Station K-7.
19. Deputy Führer of Ekos.
20. High Priestess of Yonada.
21. Leader of the Scalosians on Scalos.

22. Medicine Chief on Miramanee's Planet.

23. Leader of the Sandoval Colony on Omicron Ceti III.

24. Leader of a group of runaway slaves on Planet 892-IV.

25. Leader of the Starnes Exploration Party on Triacus.

26. Portmaster of Starbase 11.

27. Gangster Boss on Iotia.

28. Elder on Vulcan.

29. Base Commandant of Cestus III.

30. Chief Engineer of the Pergium Production Colony on Janus VI.

Your Score:

Answers to Not On Friendly Terms

1. Kohms
2. Clantons
3. Zeon
4. Vendikar
5. "The Others" (Eymorgs)
6. Oxmyx
7. Sargon
8. Bele
9. Maab
10. Troyius

Your Score:

Answers to Let Me Entertain You

1. Riley in "The Naked Time."

2. Uhura in "The Conscience of the King" and also in "The Changeling."

3. Spock in "Plato's Stepchildren."

4. Adam in "The Way to Eden."

5. Spock in "Requiem for Methusaleh."

6. Vina in "The Menagerie."

7. The children of Triacus in "And the Children Shall Lead."

8. Kirk and Spock, accompanied by Alexander, in "Plato's Stepchildren."

9. The Karidian Players in "The Conscience of the King."

10. A nameless tenor singing over the radio in "The City on the Edge of Forever."

Your Score:

Answers to "Of Great Mettle"

1. Neutronium
2. Irillium
3. Boridium
4. Dilithium Crystals
5. Beryllium-Titanium
6. Diburnium-Osmium
7. Iridium Ore
8. Rubindium
9. Duranium
10. Rodinium

Your Score:

Answers to Some Place

1. Landru's Headquarters. "The Return of the Archons"

2. Sacred place on Yonada which Natira is allowed to enter. "For the World Is Hollow and I Have Touched the Sky"

3. Also known as "The Vault of Tomorrow," the place where the horta's eggs are hatched. "The Devil in the Dark"

4. Place where the matter and the anti-matter Lazarus are destined to be forever. "The Alternative Factor"

5. Area within the Amoeba-like Creature. "The Immunity Syndrome"

6. An area of space which briefly overlaps with another area of space from a different universe. Here the crew of the *Defiant* perished and Kirk is trapped aboard the lifeless ship. "The Tholian Web"

7. A building on Ekos where Kirk, Spock, and Isak are imprisoned. "Patterns of Force"

8. "Above" is the place where the Morgs live. "Below" is the place where the Eymorgs live. Both places are on Sigma Draconis VI. "Spock's Brain"

9. Site of Dr. Janice Lester's archaeological expedition on Camus II, where one can find the Life/Entity Transfer Device. "Turnabout Intruder"

10. Place on Eminiar VII where Kirk, Spock, Yeoman Manning, Lt. Galloway, and Lt. Osborne materialize. "A Taste of Armageddon"

11. Rendezvous place on Level 23 of Janus' pergium mines where Vandenberg and his men are to combine forces with a security team from the *Enterprise*. "The Devil in the Dark"

12. Morla's address on the planet Argelius II. "Wolf in the Fold"

13. At first, the place that Kirk and the Beta III landing party are believed to be from. "The Return of the Archons"

14. Home star of the Platonians, now gone nova. "Plato's Stepchildren"

15. Place on Ardana's cloud-city of Stratos where punishment is meted out, as, for example, in the case of Vanna. "The Cloud-Minders"

Your Score:

Answers to Communications

1. Delight Lights
2. Wristlets
3. Sensor Web
4. Translator-Recorder
5. Collars of Obedience
6. Universal Translator
7. Great Teacher
8. Exceiver
9. Illusion
10. Empathic Contact

Your Score:

Answers to Poetics

1. Kirk quotes these lines from John Masefield's "Sea Fever" to McCoy in "The Ultimate Computer."

2. Parmen makes Kirk mouth these words in "Plato's Stepchildren."

3. Scott reacts out loud to a false Klingon distress signal in "Friday's Child."

4. Dr. Ozaba quotes this line from Psalm 95, Verse 4, to Dr. Linke in "The Empath."

5. Marta claims to have written A. E Housman's words in "Whom Gods Destroy."

6. Trelane addresses Yeoman Teresa Ross with Marlowe's words from *Dr. Faustus* in "The Squire of Gothos."

7. When Edith Keeler says these words to Kirk in "The City on the Edge of Forever," he tells her that they were used as the theme of a 21st century novel because its author considered their meaning even more important than the traditional "I love you."

8. Kirk quotes Shakespeare to Kelinda in "By Any Other Name."

9. McCoy and Scott recite these words in order to confuse the androids in "I, Mudd."

10. As requested by Elizabeth Dehner, Gary Mitchell recites from Tarbolde's "Nightingale Woman" (1996), a most passionate love poem, in "Where No Man Has Gone Before."

11. Spock recites from William Blake's poem after Charlie casts a spell on him in the story "Charlie X."

12. Lenore Karidian charms Kirk with these words in "The Conscience of the King."

13. Spock-Kollos uses the words of Byron to describe Uhura in "Is There in Truth No Beauty?"

14. Kirk refers to the Omicron Ceti III experience with these words in "This Side of Paradise."

15. Parmen forces Alexander to recite and perform to these lines in "Plato's Stepchildren."

Your Score:

Answers to The Amazing Mr. Spock

1. Spock reasons that the symbols represent musical notes which, when sounded, will trigger the mechanism which will open the door of the obelisk. "The Paradise Syndrome"

2. He listens, analyzes, compares, and experiments at different speeds with the tapes of the Scalosian distress call and the *Enterprise* landing party report. "Wink of an Eye"

3. Although Commodore Decker cites Starfleet Order 104, Section B, to relieve Spock of command, Spock instantly quotes from Section C, which states that a junior officer may relieve a senior officer of command on medical or psychological grounds. As a result, Spock prevents Decker from using the *Enterprise* in a self-destructive attack against the Doomsday Machine. "The Doomsday Machine"

4. Only the real Kirk would tell Spock to shoot them both. "Whom Gods Destroy"

5. Spock effects repairs on the spaceship *Yonada* and in so doing discovers the medical findings of the Fabrini, whose language he understands and is able to translate. Included in these records is the cure for McCoy's illness. "For the World Is Hollow and I Have Touched the Sky"

6. Spock adapts the Vians' Control Bar to his own brain pattern and "finds out" where McCoy is being held. "The Empath"

7. Spock discovers that the orbit of Gamma Hydra IV passed through the tail of a comet, which is the cause of all the trouble. "The Deadly Years"

8. Spock adjusts computer control so that it can't be disengaged until the ship reaches Talos IV or else all life-support systems will be cut off. "The Menagerie"

9. Spock plays five games of chess with the computer and wins all of them. He knows that this is an impossibility unless someone has been fooling around with the machine. "Court-Martial."

10. In America's "zinc-plated society" of the 1930's, the amazing Mr. Spock gets a tricorder to work and "reads" the future. "The City on the Edge of Forever"

Your Score:

Answers to What They Think

1. Spock

2. Parmen

3. Khan

4. Cochrane

5. Landru

6. McCoy

7. Nomad

8. Gorgan

9. Mitchell

10. Elaan

Your Score:

Answers to Do You Mind?

1. Spock-Kollos set a course which enables the *Enterprise* to get back to her own galaxy.

2. Spock convinces them that the Earp gang's bullets aren't real.

3. He makes Kirk forget Reena Kapec.

4. His attempt doesn't work because he picks up and is repelled by a huge, powerful, multi-tentacled creature beneath Kelinda's seemingly human form.

5. Spock can't make contact because Gem's mind doesn't function like a Vulcan's or a human's. In fact, he feels that, like a magnet, she's trying to draw things from his mind.

6. He discovers that Gill patterned Ekos after Earth's 20th century Nazi Germany because he considered it to have the most efficient organizational structure.

7. Acceding to Kirk's request, he finds out that Kirk really is trapped in Janice Lester's body.

8. He gets the guard to open the door of his cell.

9. Spock influences Sirah to pick up a communicator and signal the *Enterprise*.

10. He brings Kirk out of his state of amnesia.

11. He learns about this alien life form and the problems she's been having with the miners.

12. He finds out what has happened to Nomad since its launching.

13. He saves his own life on the operating table by telling McCoy how to proceed.

14. He learns about Dr. Adams' brain-emptying device.

15. He feels the death of 400 Vulcans.

Your Score:

Answers to By the Book I

1. F. Admiral Komack issues an order for all people on Omicron Ceti III to proceed immediately to Starbase 27 to be quarantined until they receive medical clearance. "This Side of Paradise"

2. G. The Prime Directive states that members of a landing party are not to identify themselves or their mission, interfere with the normal development of the society in which they find themselves, or refer to space, other worlds, or more advanced civilizations. In giving the Kohms phasers, Tracey violates his oath to obey the Prime Directive. "The *Omega* Glory"

3. I. This type of search presumes that the person for whom others are looking wishes to be found but is unable to respond because of some type of injury. Lt. Commander Benjamin Finney, however, does not wish to be found. "Court-Martial"

4. C. Commodore Stocker cites Regulation 7592, Section 3, Paragraph 11, in calling a hearing to determine whether Kirk is mentally and physically fit for command. "The Deadly Years"

5. B. After being taken prisoner by the Romulan Commander and sentenced to death on the charge of sabotage, Spock requests time to write his parting thoughts. "The *Enterprise* Incident"

6. H. Because he's the son of the Catullan Ambassador, Tongo Rad, one of Sevrin's "space hippies," is not brought up on charges. "The Way to Eden"

7. E. Mudd will do anything to "make a credit." This time he's acting as Cupid. "Mudd's Women"

8. J. Riley is one of the victims of a radiation sickness which is infecting the crew. When he begins acting strangely, he's told to report to Sickbay. Riley leaves Sickbay without permission and an order is issued to find and restrain him. "The Naked Time"

9. D. Baris sends this "order of orders" to Kirk to beam down immediately to Deep-Space Station K-7 to protect an important shipment of quadrotriticale. "The Trouble with Tribbles"

10. A. Marcus orders Kirk to contact the *Enterprise* to begin bringing his crew down to Planet 892-IV. Instead, Kirk communicates "Condition Green" to the ship. This code indicates trouble but prohibits those who receive it from sending help. "Bread and Circuses"

Your Score:

Answers to By the Book II

1. F. Weapons must be checked before visitors are allowed to enter penal colonies. This rule applies even to Starship Captains.

2. C. Every scientific team has to be checked once a year.

3. I. Destroy the enemy. In this case, the *Enterprise* is to wipe out Eminiar VII if Kirk doesn't succeed in his mission.

4. E. Kirk is all set to destroy the *Enterprise* and everyone aboard rather than surrender his ship to Bele.

5. A. In the Mirror Universe, no resistance is to go unpunished.

6. J. A landing party may refuse to investigate any place or culture if the investigation seems too dangerous. Kirk says he should have applied this directive on Gamma Trianguli VI.

7. G. The *Enterprise* is to proceed to Gamma 7A to find out what has happened to the *Intrepid* and why contact with her has been lost.

8. D. Spock is brought to trial on the charge of mutiny for taking over the *Enterprise* and putting her on course for Talos IV.

9. B. Reconnaissance party; rescue party; another rescue party. This is how Merik's men came down and stayed on Planet 892-IV, and, Merik says, this is how Kirk's will, too.

10. H. This is the agency Kirk recommends to Plasus and Vanna to settle their differences.

Your Score:

Answers to Ships

1. *Yorktown*
2. *Beagle*
3. *Columbia*
4. *Woden*
5. *Fesarius*
6. *Astral Queen*
7. *Excalibur*
8. *Archon*
9. *Potemkin*
10. *Horizon*

Your Score:

Answers to A. K. A.

1. Kirk on Organia
2. Flint used this name to buy Holberg 917G.
3. Mudd in "Mudd's Women"
4. Sulu tells Janice Rand that his weeper's real name is Gertrude, not Beauregard as she's been calling the plant.
5. Dr. Roger Korby
6. Edith Keeler
7. Dr. Leonard McCoy
8. This is just one of the M-113 Creature's aliases.
9. William B. Harrison, late Flight Officer of the *U. S. Beagle*
10. Surak
11. The real Nancy Crater's nickname for McCoy.
12. Eymorgs
13. Apollo
14. Kara
15. Elaan, Dohlman of Elas

Your Score:

Answers to Romantic Interludes

1. Lt. Mira Romaine is a specialist in charge of supervising the newly-designed equipment which the *Enterprise* is transporting to Memory Alpha. "The Lights of Zetar"

2. Reena Kapec, Flint's ward, is really an android. "Requiem for Methusaleh"

3. Droxine is the beautiful daughter of Plasus. She is an intellectual who lives in the cloud-city of Stratos. "The Cloud-Minders"

4. Janice Lester is the power-hungry doctor who uses the life-transference machine to change bodies with Kirk. "Turnabout Intruder"

5. Janice Rand is a yeoman aboard the *Enterprise*. She's also the first girl Charlie has ever seen. "Charlie X"

6. Elizabeth Dehner, a psychiatrist, offers her life on behalf of Gary. "Where No Man Has Gone Before"

7. Dr. Roger Korby, an archaeologist, has preserved himself as an android. He and Christine were once engaged. "What Are Little Girls Made Of?"

8. Mira chooses Compton to be her mate in the hyperaccelerated world of Scalos. Unfortunately, he dies shortly after his arrival. "Wink of an Eye"

9. Vina, who has been given the illusion of beauty by the Talosians, sees Pike as the "perfect specimen." Pike returns to Talos and Vina after he has been disfigured in an explosion. He, too, needs his illusion. "The Menagerie"

10. Tonia Barrows accompanies McCoy to the "Pleasure Planet." He is struck by her beauty and is given the opportunity of defending her honor. McCoy is "slain" and then "restored to life." "Shore Leave"

11. After many years of not seeing him, Areel Shaw, one of Kirk's former girlfriends, shows up as the lawyer for the prosecution in Kirk's trial. "Court-Martial"

12. Spock is the object of the Romulan Commander's attentions. In her attempts to attract him, she even changes from her uniform into a dress. Spock does notice! "The *Enterprise* Incident"

13. Drusilla is Proconsul Claudius Marcus' slave. He lends her to Kirk to make his last hours of life more comfortable. "Bread and Circuses"

14. Irini Galliulin was Chekov's sweetheart when they were students at Starfleet Academy. Now she's a "space hippie." "The Way to Eden"

15. Odona, who is on a mission of self-sacrifice, finds herself so strongly attracted to Kirk that she would like him to remain on Gideon. After he leaves, the memory of how she has come to

share Kirk's immunity to Vegan chloriomeningitis lingers on. "The Mark of Gideon"

16. Spock has a special place in Christine Chapel's life. Once they shared consciousness. "Return to Tomorrow"; another time he kissed her—although Parmen made him do it. "Plato's Stepchildren"; and in "The Naked Time," she even confessed her love to him. Alas, their relationship is all one-sided!

17. Marta and Garth are both inmates of the galaxy's only insane asylum. Theirs is a very strange relationship, for although Garth has chosen Marta to be his consort, he knowingly sends her to her death. "Whom Gods Destroy"

18. Kirk is the victim of Elaan's tears. Even though he loves her, he loves the *Enterprise* more, and she resigns herself to becoming the wife of the Troyian ruler. "Elaan of Troyius"

19. Spock meets Zarabeth more than 6,000 years in her planet's past. He falls in love with her and reluctantly returns to the present. "All Our Yesterdays"

20. Chekov is most protective of Yeoman Martha Landon on Gamma Trianguli VI. They seem to have something going! "The Apple"

Your Score:

Answers to To Catch a Thief

1. Lokai

2. Spock

3. Dr. Sevrin's "space hippies"

4. Kirk

5. Jahn

6. Dr. Sevrin's "space hippies"

7. The horta

8. Kara

9. Both the matter and the anti-matter Lazarus

10. Kirk

Your Score:

Answers to Not to Be Believed

1. As a result of radiation sickness, Kirk is aging rapidly and suffering memory loss. He means to say Gamma Hydra IV.

2. Hodin plans on using Kirk to infect Gideon's disease-free population; therefore, he lies to Spock in the hope that Spock will believe him and leave with the *Enterprise*. Spock, however, discerns the discrepancy in the transporter coordinates which were beamed up from the planet: the first was 875; 020; 079 for Kirk's trip down to Gideon; the second was 875; 020; 709 for the Gideonite who was beamed aboard the *Enterprise*. Needless to say, Spock goes to Kirk's rescue.

3. Kirk advances this reason in order to be captured and taken aboard the Romulan ship so that he can figure out a way to steal the Romulan cloaking device.

4. Spock temporarily overlooks the fact that Christopher's son, Shaun Geoffrey, is to make a significant contribution in the area of space development; therefore, Christopher has to be sent back to Earth because his son hasn't been conceived yet.

5. Kirk doesn't really die. Spock's nerve pinch simulates death.

6. Kirk did no such thing. Finney tampered with the computer tape in an attempt to "get even" with Kirk. Finney is still alive but obviously not too well mentally.

7. Kirk asked Scott to lie deliberately in order to show how sensitive the computer is to fact and fiction.

8. Spock correctly identifies the ship as a DY 100.

9. Septimus and his followers really worship the Son, meaning the Son of God.

10. Not a word of truth here! The "victims" of Eminiar VII's computerized war with Vendikar are expected to surrender their lives and property instantly and obediently.

Your Score:

Answers to How Distressing!

1. Parmen from Platonius
    "Plato's Stepchildren"

2. Khan and all aboard the *Botany Bay*
    "Space Seed"

3. The Scalosians (especially the women)
    "Wink of an Eye"

4. Miri's Planet
    "Miri"

5. Nilz Baris gets Mr. Lurry all upset on Deep-Space Station K-7.
    "The Trouble with Tribbles"

6. Sargon
    "Return to Tomorrow"

7. Dr. Janice Lester
    "Turnabout Intruder"

8. Rojan
    "By Any Other Name"

9. The Pergium Production Colony on Janus VI
    "The Devil in the Dark"

10. The Energy Entity
    "Day of the Dove"

Your Score:

Answers to Drink It In

1.	Finagle's Folly	"The Ultimate Computer"
2.	Milk	"Bread and Circuses"
3.	Rice Wine	"The Enemy Within"
4.	Vodka	"The Trouble with Tribbles"
5.	A bottle of Scotch	"Is There in Truth No Beauty?"
6.	A glass of Saurian brandy	"Requiem for Methusaleh"
7.	Bourbon	"Spectre of the Gun"
8.	Scalosian water	"Wink of an Eye"
9.	Trova	"A Taste of Armageddon"
10.	Tranya	"The Corbomite Maneuver"

Your Score:

Answers to Name Calling

1. This is Charlie's name for Spock. "Charlie X"

2. The Children of Triacus address Gorgan in this way.
    "And the Children Shall Lead"

3. Anton Karidian was given this epithet by the people when
    he was Governor Kodos of Taurus IV.
    "The Conscience of the King"

4. This is Kirk's name for Commodore Stocker.
    "The Deadly Years"

5. The Melkots use this uncomplimentary term to describe the
    Enterprise and her crew. "Spectre of the Gun"

6. Rodent refers to Edith Keeler by this name.
    "The City on the Edge of Forever"

7. Zefram Cochrane uses this name to describe himself.
    "Metamorphosis"

8. The matter Lazarus describes the anti-matter Lazarus in this way.
    "The Alternative Factor"

9. This is one of Korax's names for Kirk.
    "The Trouble with Tribbles"

10. Christine Chapel describes Korby's creation of a female
    android named Andrea in this manner.
    "What Are Little Girls Made Of?"

Your Score:

Answers to The One and Only

1. The horta
2. Norman
3. Vulcan
4. Quadrotriticale
5. McCoy
6. Tribbles
7. Kirk
8. Lt. Harold
9. T'Pau
10. Vina
11. Marlena Moreau
12. The M-113 Creature
13. Charlie Evans
14. Tombstone, Arizona, Melkotian style
15. Spock

Your Score:

Answers to "Expert-Tease"

1. The now extinct natives of Exo III.
2. The incorporeal "Companion" assumed Nancy Hedford's body as the latter died.
3. To Colony 5
4. Gamma II
5. Marplon
6. Mavig
7. Ensign Freeman
8. Thelev
9. Schmitter
10. "No kill I."
11. On a helium experimental station.
12. "The Final Solution"
13. Floyd's
14. Clark Gable
15. *The Star Dispatch*
16. Coridan's admission to the Federation
17. Pavel Andreievich Chekov
18. The credit
19. The Metrons
20. Kirk had a medical rest leave.
21. Scott
22. Hacom
23. The Guardian of Forever
24. The quatloo.
25. "Kirk to *Enterprise*"
26. "Live long and prosper."
27. The transmuter

28. Tamoon
29. "LOVE MANKIND" and "SINNER REPENT," respectively
30. Freedom
31. It set a precedent in interstellar law.
32. "Queen to King's level one."
33. Yeoman Tankris
34. First he destroyed the memory banks in Directional Control and Self-Destruct and then his will took over the ship.
35. Hodgkin's Law of Parallel Planet Development
36. That he was hungry.
37. *U. S. S. Republic*
38. *The Book of the People*
39. Kor
40. Trillium and kevas
41. Double Jack
42. Colored gelatin
43. Starbase 2
44. In accordance with his own Vulcan philosophy, he won't put his father's life before Starfleet Rules and Regulations.
45. Harcourt Fenton Mudd
46. He illegally sold the rights to a Vulcan fuel synthesizer.
47. Once every 11 years.
48. One which is able to support human life without artificial means.
49. Samuel T. Cogley
50. Dr. Roger Korby's assistant, Dr. Brown, whom Christine had always called "Brownie." (This nickname hadn't been programmed into his android form.)
51. Gary Seven
52. Fizzbin

53. Tiburon
54. Tan Ru
55. Mirrored discs
56. The Great Teacher or The Great Teacher of All the Ancient Knowledge.
57. Jack the Ripper
58. The 23rd century
59. Spock saved his life.
60. An odor
61. Thermoconcrete
62. Abraham Lincoln
63. Tomar
64. Leonard James Akaar
65. Angela Martine
66. Whining mosquito sounds
67. Rot
68. Tricorder
69. Manual override.
70. Sea ranch
71. An echo
72. By placing her in a pressure chamber.
73. The Body
74. A UFO
75. McCoy
76. Lal or Thann
77. Andromeda

Your Score:

Solution to Who Knows Where?

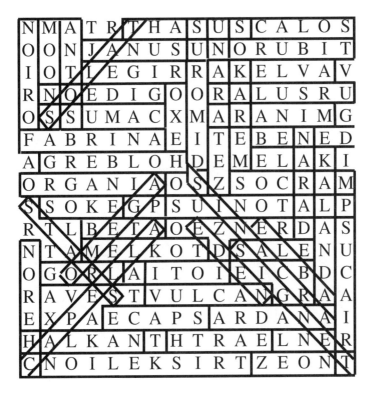

Your Score:

Solution to The *Enterprise*

```
D U C T F A R C E L T T U H S
E N E R G I Z E J R E W O P R
C C L E A R E T T A M D A T E
K H O L D C R E D R O C I R T
T A A A S H I P E W E I V E R
R N O I C A I G U N X R J E O
O N T E L P R A W T I C N L P
P E T Z E E N A C S T U B E S
P L R O B L A B K E R I W V N
U M A N L A E E S N B T F A A
S H I E L D N G E F A N D T R
E E N R U A G D N Z S I I O T
F L I G H T I I S A E B O R P
I M R A L A N R O A R A D A R
L G O L M A E B R O T C A R T
```

Your Score:

Your Score for Role Playing (Opposite Page):

Solution to Role Playing

Part IV: Scorecard

Scorecard
(1460 points)

1314 or more points: "True Trekker"

1168 - 1313 points: "Out of This World"

1022 - 1167 points: "Starry-Eyed"

876 - 1021 points: "On the Right Trek"

Below 876 points: "Earthbound"

Part V: Appendices

Appendix I

Alphabetical Listing of The Episodes

1. "A Piece of the Action"
2. "A Private Little War"
3. "A Taste of Armageddon"
4. "All Our Yesterdays"
5. "Amok Time"
6. "And the Children Shall Lead"
7. "Arena"
8. "Assignment: Earth"
9. "Balance of Terror"
10. "Bread and Circuses"
11. "By Any Other Name"
12. "Catspaw"
13. "Charlie X"
14. "Court-Martial"
15. "Dagger of the Mind"
16. "Day of the Dove"
17. "Elaan of Troyius"
18. "Errand of Mercy"
19. "For the World Is Hollow and I Have Touched the Sky"
20. "Friday's Child"
21. "I, Mudd"

22. "Is There in Truth No Beauty?"
23. "Journey to Babel"
24. "Let That Be Your Last Battlefield"
25. "Metamorphosis"
26. "Miri"
27. "Mirror, Mirror"
28. "Mudd's Women"
29. "Obsession"
30. "Operation: Annihilate!"
31. "Patterns of Force"
32. "Plato's Stepchildren"
33. "Requiem for Methusaleh"
34. "Return to Tomorrow"
35. "Shore Leave"
36. "Space Seed"
37. "Spectre of the Gun"
38. "Spock's Brain"
39. "That Which Survives"
40. "The Alternative Factor"
41. "The Apple"
42. "The Changeling"
43. "The City on the Edge of Forever"
44. "The Cloud-Minders"
45. "The Conscience of the King"

46.   "The Corbomite Maneuver"
47.   "The Deadly Years"
48.   "The Devil in the Dark"
49.   "The Doomsday Machine"
50.   "The Empath"
51.   "The Enemy Within"
52.   "The *Enterprise* Incident"
53.   "The *Galileo* Seven"
54.   "The Gamesters of Triskelion"
55.   "The Immunity Syndrome"
56.   "The Lights of Zetar"
57.   "The Man Trap"
58.   "The Mark of Gideon"
59.   "The Menagerie"
60.   "The Naked Time"
61.   "The *Omega* Glory"
62.   "The Paradise Syndrome"
63.   "The Return of the Archons"
64.   "The Savage Curtain"
65.   "The Squire of Gothos"
66.   "The Tholian Web"
67.   "The Trouble with Tribbles"
68.   "The Ultimate Computer"
69.   "The Way to Eden"

70. "This Side of Paradise"
71. "Tomorrow Is Yesterday"
72. "Turnabout Intruder"
73. "What Are Little Girls Made Of?"
74. "Where No Man Has Gone Before"
75. "Who Mourns for Adonais?"
76. "Whom Gods Destroy"
77. "Wink of an Eye"
78. "Wolf in the Fold"

Appendix II

Chronological Listing Of The Episodes By Stardate

1.	Unknown	"Assignment: Earth"
2.	Unknown	"Day of the Dove"
3.	Unknown	"Mirror, Mirror"
4.	Unknown	"That Which Survives"
5.	Unknown	"The *Omega* Glory"
6.	1312.4	"Where No Man Has Gone Before"
7.	1329.8	"Mudd's Women"
8.	1512.2	"The Corbomite Maneuver"
9.	1513.1	"The Man Trap"
10.	1533.7	"Charlie X"
11.	1672.1	"The Enemy Within"
12.	1704.2	"The Naked Time"
13.	1709.1	"Balance of Terror"
14.	2124.5	"The Squire of Gothos"
15.	2534.0	"Patterns of Force"
16.	2712.4	"What Are Little Girls Made Of?"
17.	2713.5	"Miri"
18.	2715.1	"Dagger of the Mind"
19.	2817.6	"The Conscience of the King"
20.	2821.5	"The *Galileo* Seven"
21.	2947.3*	"Court-Martial"

22.	3012.4	"The Menagerie"
23.	3018.2	"Catspaw"
24.	3025.3	"Shore Leave"
25.	3045.6	"Arena"
26.	3087.6	"The Alternative Factor"
27.	3113.2	"Tomorrow Is Yesterday"
28.	3134.0	"The City on the Edge of Forever"
29.	3141.9	"Space Seed"
30.	3156.2	"The Return of the Archons"
31.	3192.1	"A Taste of Armageddon"
32.	3196.1	"The Devil in the Dark"
33.	3198.4	"Errand of Mercy"
34.	3211.7	"The Gamesters of Triskelion"
35.	3219.8	"Metamorphosis"
36.	3287.2	"Operation: Annihilate!"
37.	3372.7	"Amok Time"
38.	3417.3	"This Side of Paradise"
39.	3468.1	"Who Mourns for Adonais?"
40.	3478.2	"The Deadly Years"
41.	3497.2	"Friday's Child"
42.	3541.9	"The Changeling"
43.	3614.9	"Wolf in the Fold"
44.	3619.2	"Obsession"
45.	3715.3	"The Apple"

46.	3842.3	"Journey to Babel"
47.	4040.7	"Bread and Circuses"
48.	4202.9**	"The Doomsday Machine"
49.	4211.4	"A Private Little War"
50.	4307.1	"The Immunity Syndrome"
51.	4372.5	"Elaan of Troyius"
52.	4385.3	"Spectre of the Gun"
53.	4513.3	"I, Mudd"
54.	4523.3	"The Trouble with Tribbles"
55.	4598.0	"A Piece of the Action"
56.	4657.5	"By Any Other Name"
57.	4729.4	"The Ultimate Computer"
58.	4768.3	"Return to Tomorrow"
59.	4842.6	"The Paradise Syndrome"
60.	5027.3	"The *Enterprise* Incident"
61.	5029.5	"And the Children Shall Lead"
62.	5121.5	"The Empath"
63.	5423.4	"The Mark of Gideon"
64.	5431.4	"Spock's Brain"
65.	5476.3	"For the World Is Hollow and I Have Touched the Sky"
66.	5630.7	"Is There in Truth No Beauty?"
67.	5693.2	"The Tholian Web"
68.	5710.5	"Wink of an Eye"

69.	5718.3	"Whom Gods Destroy"
70.	5725.3	"The Lights of Zetar"
71.	5730.2	"Let That Be Your Last Battlefield"
72.	5784.2	"Plato's Stepchildren"
73.	5818.4	"The Cloud-Minders"
74.	5832.3	"The Way to Eden"
75.	5843.7	"Requiem for Methusaleh"
76.	5906.4	"The Savage Curtain"
77.	5928.5	"Turnabout Intruder"
78.	5943.7	"All Our Yesterdays"

*The action goes back to 2945.7

**The action goes back to 4202.1

This book was meant to be accurate and clear. We welcome comments from all Trekkers. Please send inquiries or orders to:

Mayhaven Publishing
P O Box 557
Mahomet, IL 61853